Key Research Concepts in
Politics & International Relations

The SAGE Key Concepts series provides students with accessible and authoritative knowledge of the essential topics in a variety of disciplines. Cross-referenced throughout, the format encourages critical evaluation through understanding. Written by experienced and respected academics, the books are indispensable study aids and guides to comprehension.

Key Research Concepts in
Politics & International Relations

LISA HARRISON & THERESA CALLAN

Los Angeles | London | New Delhi
Singapore | Washington DC

Los Angeles | London | New Delhi
Singapore | Washington DC

SAGE Publications Ltd
1 Oliver's Yard
55 City Road
London EC1Y 1SP

SAGE Publications Inc.
2455 Teller Road
Thousand Oaks, California 91320

SAGE Publications India Pvt Ltd
B 1/I 1 Mohan Cooperative Industrial Area
Mathura Road
New Delhi 110 044

SAGE Publications Asia-Pacific Pte Ltd
3 Church Street
#10-04 Samsung Hub
Singapore 049483

Editor: Natalie Aguilera
Editorial assistant: James Piper
Production editor: Katie Forsythe
Copyeditor: Roza El-Eini
Proofreader: Clare Weaver
Marketing manager: Sally Ransom
Typeset by: C&M Digitals (P) Ltd, Chennai, India
Printed in India at Replika Press, Pvt Ltd

First published 2013

Library of Congress Control Number: 2012938114

British Library Cataloguing in Publication data

A catalogue record for this book is available from
the British Library

ISBN 978-1-4129-1184-9
ISBN 978-1-4129-1185-6 (pbk)

contents

contents

v

key research concepts in
politics & international relations

about the authors

Lisa Harrison is a political scientist who specializes in researching electoral politics in the UK, and producing student-focused materials for political research methods. She has published in journals such as *Political Quarterly*, *Parliamentary Affairs* and *The Journal of Legislative Studies* and is a regular commentator in the media. Her interest in teaching and learning issues in politics has led to a number of publications. For several years she has been a member of the Political Studies Association UK Executive Committee and is a passionate advocate of the study, and clear communication, of politics as an academic discipline.

Theresa Callan is a political scientist who specializes in security politics, specifically ethnic conflict and post-conflict peacebuilding, and international relations theory, specifically realist perspectives. She also teaches and develops material on research methods and study skills, with a special interest in ontological questions and grammar (much to the delight of her students). A member of the Political Studies Association and the British International Studies Association, she is dedicated to the teaching of politics in an inclusive, engaged way and has a special distaste for osbscurantist practices.

introduction

This book has been written as a contribution to the SAGE Key Concepts series, but, more importantly for us, we have produced something that we hope students will find an important resource throughout their studies.

Research methods are rarely the key reason for people choosing to study Politics or International Relations, yet they are recognized as a crucial element in any such degree. Just as we would expect to learn about political theory and explore examples of political case studies, we recognize that good graduates need to have a toolkit of skills to assist in answering 'Who?', 'What?', 'Where?' and 'When?' questions.

The discipline of Politics was lamentably slow in explicitly embedding research methods into the curriculum or providing suitable texts and guides in comparison to subjects such as Psychology and Sociology (and International Relations even more so!). Thankfully, this began to change in the 1990s and there are some excellent political research methods textbooks that take students through the process of research – many of which we reference.

By producing a Key Concepts guide, we have attempted to do something slightly different. We have focused on commonly employed concepts that students often struggle to understand and, at times, misuse. For each concept, we offer a succinct explanation that is cross-referenced to related concepts. In order to escape some of the 'dryness' often associated with political research methods we also, where appropriate, signpost the reader towards studies that engage with the concept. In doing so we wanted to show that what we know about politics and international relations *cannot* be explained without understanding the research process by means of which 'knowledge' is generated. A fundamental reason why we disagree about political explanations is because we ask different questions in different ways. Political researchers privilege different methodologies and methods – we do not make judgements here about which are 'better' or 'best', but we do believe that by recognizing such differences we develop a clearer understanding of why competing arguments survive and thrive.

Each concept is focused and intended to be illustrative. We cross-reference other concepts where possible and supplement each entry with two types of bibliography. Further reading will take you to sources that explore the concept in further detail. Examples feature published research that engages with the concept to some degree – to us these are exemplars of research in the fields of politics and international relations as they are explicit in raising methodological issues emerging from the research process (either intentionally or accidentally).

Inevitably in preparing a text of this nature we have not been able to cover every concept – apologies if you are seeking something we chose not to include. The content was guided by proposal reviewers and our own experiences of teaching – we have found that students are often baffled by the chosen key concepts in terms of both their meaning and application.

We are grateful for Dr Jamie Munn's early input (regarding the concepts of action research, case studies, feminism, narratives, positivism and post-positivism), in addition to those colleagues, family, friends and supportive staff at SAGE who have all helped in seeing this project through to completion.

Finally, we hope that students will engage with the content – and feel that the challenging discipline of research methods is a little less mystifying than they thought it might be!

introduction

Action Research

Action research is not to be confused with **case study** research. In action research, researchers test and refine principles, tools and **methodologies** to address *real-world* problems.

It is a characteristic of action research that the participants or 'practitioners' as well as the researchers participate in the analysis, design and implementation processes and usually add as much as the researchers to any decision-making. It can be said to create a *synergy* between the practitioners and the researcher as they test, modify and test again research ideas for solving *real-world* problems. The flow of continual feedback used to modify the tests encourages positive information and discussions between the two, so that the test and the research questions can be improved on and developed.

The purpose of the research – to provide new data and information for the practitioners – also can change with the development of the reinvention of the testing that results from the increasing awareness of both researcher and practitioner. Thus, whereas case study research examines phenomena in their 'natural' environment with the researcher as an independent (separate) observer, in action research the researcher ought to be useful as well as an observer.

Action research, then, is a form of experiments based on the new developments that come out of the reinvention of the original test and research questions. For those researchers interested in **qualitative methods**, this approach allows them to use research that consists of first-hand experiences, people's stories guiding the aims of good research to solve real-world problems while dealing with localized contingencies. Action research involves using participatory methods as much as possible. As the researcher and practitioner modify the experiment at each stage, they could reach different outcomes from what is being achieved as a result of the modifications.

If we take an example, we could argue that, in the world of political policy development, the practitioner may not come from a research background and therefore needs the assistance of the researcher to discover public opinion or develop the projection of political policy. This format also often stresses the necessity of moving relatively quickly

action research

1

towards *new* action. The informality and interpretive (experimental) nature of this methodology encourages the collaboration between participant and researcher. It is because of this relationship that action research is often carried out by those who already recognize there is a problem or limitation within their subject and intend for the research project to bring those involved together in a manner that will facilitate and reflect on outcomes. As such, effective action research is associated with experienced researchers.

The key thing to remember about action research is it is intended to be a developmental tool and method that allows the researcher to reflect and then act. An example here may help to illustrate the action research process. When undertaking a piece of research, we often follow the conventional process of setting a question (hypothesis), developing a fieldwork study, analysing that study and drawing out the conclusions. This process proceeds from point A to point B in a linear push, whereas action research involves a cycle of action, reflection, the development of questions, the mapping out and review of past and current actions, drawing in the experiences of the participants/practitioners. The process continues by developing some conclusions at these stages and then setting a course of new actions. It is important to note here that this cycle does not end but often continues with the practitioners (and sometimes the researcher) reflecting again on the new actions and moving through the system once again, which is then further researched.

The differences between action research and the conventional process are not necessarily about it being a 'new' kind of research method, but, rather, in terms of the involvement and consideration of those implementing and participating in the 'day-to-day' actions or practices. It makes sense to assume that all research is an implementation of action. Research in itself is an action involving current problems or situations and, as a result of this, researchers have to keep in mind that their involvement always has consequences.

Action research, by definition, operates at the social level and, thus, researchers are aware that interventions and changes will have to be made in the process. Most action research is designed to look into a particular situation, policy or scenario in order to change it or improve it. It makes sense that those involved in a situation that is seen to be unsatisfactory will wish to alter it for the better and also ought to be included in the process of developing new actions. However, it is not always the case that action research springs out of an unsatisfactory situation. It can be used to replicate or add to an experience that works well. For example, a winning economic development project or a strong campaign strategy can be examined in order to test its success in a new setting or when used by a different organizational group.

In action research, even though there is a conceptual difference between the 'action', the 'research' and the 'participation' involved, such differences begin to disappear during the research project itself. Remember, there is not a linear push through the project (participation + research = action). Instead, there are cycles of reflection on actions (past and present), followed by new actions that then themselves become the subject of reflection. The hallmark of action research is that change does not happen at the end of the research project but throughout it.

FURTHER READING

Coghlan, D. (2005) *Doing Action Research in your Own Organization* (2nd edn). London: Sage.

EXAMPLES

Burgess, J. (2006) 'Participatory action research: First-person perspectives of a graduate student', *Action Research*, 4 (4): 419–37.

Coghlan, D. and Shani, A. (2005) 'Roles, politics, and ethics in action research design', *Systemic Practice and Action Research*, 18 (6): 533–46.

Kenny, S. (1994) *Developing Communities for the Future*. Melbourne: Thomas Nelson.

Wakeford, T. and Pimbert, M. (2004) 'Prajateerpu, power and knowledge: The politics of participatory action research in development', *Action Research*, 2 (1): 25–46.

Autobiographical/ Biographical Research

Autobiographical and biographical research (BR) are interpretivist **qualitative methods** usually sited within the **narrative** research tradition. Such research has a long history, with antecedents such as Plutarch's

Parallel Lives and Suetonius' *The Twelve Caesars*. Arguably, contemporary autobiographical and biographical works do not have such august status. Current output tends to flow from erstwhile celebrities (or their 'ghostwriters') from the worlds of sport, music, reality TV, talk shows and 'life coaching'. All contribute, sometimes repeatedly, to what Pimlott (1999: 31) has termed 'a biographical bottleneck'. Perhaps due to this celebrity-dominated industry, and its largely ephemeral nature, autobiographical and biographical research tends to be viewed as a neglected and 'disciplinary poor relation' in political research (Pimlott, 1990: 224). Such neglect, however, occurs at the researcher's peril.

Biographical research is the gathering and interpretation of an array of material or 'documents of life' (Plummer, 2001). Such life artefacts come in varied written forms, such as autobiographies, biographies, diaries, letters, speeches and policy statements, as well as in visual and aural forms, such as photographs and visual and oral recordings. In political research, sources also include *Hansard* and other public records, Cabinet or committee meetings and so on. The range of sources available reflects the breadth of this research approach.

Biographical research is found in different academic disciplines, such as history, sociology and literary studies. The different disciplines have their specific approaches to using biographical material, but all share an appreciation that such material may help 'to reveal and understand the "personal" and its interlinking with the immediate and wider social context and political practices' (Roberts, 2002: 31).

Political researchers can use life documents to uncover and explain the background to specific decisions, why leaders acted as they did and why certain policies were chosen over others – albeit some very recent autobiographical and biographical accounts seem more drawn to settling scores and revealing 'pyscho-dramas' in the corridors of power than anything else. As such, it may be useful for researchers to distinguish between the speedy 'my story' type of BR and that resulting from a lengthier wait.

Essentially, biographical research allows for a fuller appreciation of human agency and its context at the heart of politics. It helps to evince a better understanding of Lasswell's (1936) who gets what, when, and how. The context in which the individual subject stands is 'the real meat of the story' and a good biography 'illuminates a changing environment by revealing the way in which a particular character interacts with it' (Pimlott, 1999: 39). Such a biography, then, operates simultaneously at two levels: the micro level of the individual and the wider, social level. Given its usefulness, the underdeployment of autobiographical and biographical approaches in political research needs to be explained. This mainly stems from concerns about the **validity**, accuracy and **reliability** of biographical material.

Due to the interpretivist nature of this approach, the 'outputs' are not readily quantifiable as they are more a case of subjectivity and understanding. The anti-positivist nature of biographical research leads to the criticism that it is an unreliable approach, giving rise to a mixture of fact and fiction, known as 'faction'. Thus, when dealing with life documents, the researcher needs to reflect on what drove 'the autobiographical impulse', what prompted the subject to write that account, to keep a diary, to compose a letter and so on. The motivation needs to be considered as it could well have influenced the subject's recollection and recording of the event/issue concerned. The prospect of a future audience reading an autobiography or diaries, for example, may prompt authors to cast themselves in a more benign light and/or to be, say, a little economical with the actualité. As public figures, especially politicians and their key aides, seem in an almost indecent rush to get their accounts out into the public domain, we might well wonder at the validity of their respective interpretations of events and their roles in them.

When writing biographies, researchers may become too close to their subjects and succumb to 'transference' – overidentifying with them and becoming 'so enamoured of their subject, warts and all, that they sometimes lose their sense of proportion' (Pimlott, 1999: 38). Biography writers may face ethical dilemmas, such as to what extent, if any, they should make known private peccadilloes. They may face difficulties in securing access to biographical material, particularly if it is held by a gatekeeper who wishes to manage the perception of the subject. Subjectivity, then, both in terms of editing and access, affects the composition of a biography. If the subject of the work is alive and cooperative, then he or she can assist with matters of clarification (albeit subjectively bounded, of course). Ultimately, however, whether the author is the subject (an autobiographer) or not (a biographer), the life materials will be subjectively selected and interpreted. Given this degree of latitude, '[b]oth autobiography and biography, then, contain the potential for bias and distortion' (McNeill and Chapman, 2005: 152).

The aim of biographical research, though, is to construct a narrative – an impressionistic representation rather than any unassailable 'truth'. The core of the accounts may be tested through comparison with other contemporaneous accounts or data, but they must not be regarded as neutral sources. Their subjectivity warrants caution in their use, but does not

autobiographical/
biographical research

5

render them useless. Increasingly, the biographical approach has been widened to include more than the life materials of 'great men of history' that reinforce a 'top-down' view of politics. Feminist research programmes have used biographical and autobiographical materials to give volume to the voices of women and those from 'below stairs' and to present a fuller picture both of individual lives and wider sociopolitical contexts (Stanley, 1992). The biographical approach may also be seen in recent work on the politics of memory and in the field of migration studies.

FURTHER READING

Lasswell, H. (1936) Politics: Who Gets What, When, How? New York: McGraw-Hill.
McNeill, P. and Chapman, S. (2005) *Research Methods* (3rd edn). Abingdon: Routledge.
Pimlott, B. (1990) 'The future of political biography', *Political Quarterly*, 61 (2): 214–24.
Pimlott, B. (1999) 'Is contemporary biography history?', *Political Quarterly*, 70 (1): 31–41.
Plummer, K. (2001) *Documents of Life 2: An invitation to critical humanism*. London: Sage.
Roberts, B. (2002) *Biographical Research*. Buckingham: Open University Press.
Stanley, L. (1992) *The Autobiographical I: The theory and practice of feminist autobiography*. Manchester: Manchester University Press.

EXAMPLES

Blair, T. (2010) *A Journey*. London: Hutchinson/Random House Group.
Humphrey, R., Miller, R. and Zdravomyslova, E. (eds) (2003) *Biographical Research in Eastern Europe: Altered lives and broken biographies*. Aldershot, Hampshire: Ashgate.
Mullin, C. (2009) *Decline and Fall: Diaries 2005–2010*. London: Profile Books.
Wheen, F. (1999) *Karl Marx: A life*. New York: W.W. Norton & Co.

.... Behaviouralism ....

An explanation of the centrality of behaviouralism to debates on research **methodology** in political science is unavoidable – given its salience in debates surrounding the preference for positivist versus interpretivist traditions. However, behaviouralism did not arise merely as a response to philosophical debates in politics but also to the nineteenth- and early twentieth-century dominance of institutionalism – in which much of political research focused on formal political institutions and organizations, such as constitutions, legislatures and bureaucracies. 'The clear message was that there was much, much more to politics than the formal arrangements for representation, decision-making and policy implementation' (Lowndes, 2002: 90). Furthermore, we can see links with other disciplines – behavioural psychology being one such example. However, behaviouralism was not just driven by the preference for particular approaches but also by the research opportunities facilitated by developments in **methods**, including **survey design**, sampling and the collection of large-scale **quantitative** data.

Sanders (2002: 45) emphasizes the positivist elements of a behaviouralist approach:

- it focuses on what is observable (at the individual and aggregate level)
- explanations of behaviour should be subject to empirical testing

In order to generate what Sanders refers to as 'good' theories, it is important that *all* relevant empirical data is explored rather than 'a limited set of illustrative examples' – this addresses accusations of anecdotal research. Of course, when studying large research populations that cannot feasibly be accessed in total (such as eligible voters), then the relevant data has to embody notions of representativeness (see **sampling**). Central, then, to the behavioural approach is the process of **hypothesis testing** and the testing of statements that are falsifiable.

Kavanagh (1983) points to the link between behaviouralism and the so-called 'Americanization' of political science and, indeed, it is still the case that political *scientist* is a label more commonly used in American universities (see Marsh and Savigny, 2004) than elsewhere. The early, so-called 'classics' of political behaviouralism have provided models that have been tested – both over time and across nations and cultures. These include:

- Almond and Verba (1963) *The Civic Culture* – this study of political values, feelings and beliefs enabled the authors to identify links between types of political culture (parochial, subject and participant) and the stability of liberal democracy

- Lazarsfeld et al. (1944) *The People's Choice* – the first large-scale survey study of voting behaviour in the USA, which emphasized the relationship between social characteristics (such as class, religion and race) and voter preferences. The first British study – Butler and Stokes (1969) *Political Change in Britain* – also emphasized the importance of social class.

However, this strong and continued association with political science does not mean that behaviouralism has little to offer those specializing in international relations. For example, Jordan (2003) utilizes an 'oral testimony approach' (that is, interviews with a range of peaceworkers) and a multicultural perspective to examine the role of women working in conflict areas in transformational peacemaking processes.

Sanders identifies three general criticisms of the behavioural approach:

- It is subject to the same weaknesses as positivism – underplaying the significance of normative, aesthetic and moral arguments. While these debates may not be central to behavioural analysis, this does not mean that behaviouralists reject the importance of such studies per se, but 'scholars working in non-empirical traditions are never able to provide a satisfactory answer to the crucial question: "How would you know if you were wrong?"' (2002: 51)
- By focusing on the observable, certain phenomena are marginalized by behaviouralists. Indeed, we know that some questions are much more profound and difficult to answer than others, yet they may be just as relevant to understanding political motivations and actions than the 'measurable' variables that behaviouralists prefer. Furthermore, there is a tendency to focus on the individual as it is easier to observe the preferences of people rather than groups or states – the latter of which are much more prominent in international relations research than particular individuals (except in the case of elites).
- In its formative era, behaviouralists assumed a level of independence between theory and observation. While theoretical understandings can impact upon the observations we set out to make, behaviouralists defend the potential for relativism by claiming that their justification of a 'good' theory is whether or not it is supported by empirical observation. A way of phrasing this may be 'we all ask slightly different questions, but whether or not we choose to believe arguments rests on evidence of reliability and validity that we can have a shared understanding of'.

FURTHER READING

Kavanagh, D. (1983) *Political Science and Political Behaviour*. London: Allen & Unwin.

Marsh, D. and Savigny, H. (2004) 'Political science as a broad church: The search for a pluralist discipline', *Politics*, 24 (3): 155–68.

Sanders, D. (2002) 'Behaviouralism', in D. Marsh and G. Stoker (eds), *Theory and Methods in Political Science* (2nd edn). Houndmills, Basingstoke: Palgrave Macmillan.

EXAMPLES

Almond, G. and Verba, S. (1963) *The Civic Culture*. Princeton, NJ: Princeton University Press.

Butler, D. and Stokes, D. (1969) *Political Change in Britain*. Houndmills, Basingstoke: Palgrave Macmillan.

Jordan, A. (2003) 'Women and conflict transformation: Influences, roles, and experiences', *Development in Practice*, 13 (2–3): 239–52.

Lazarsfeld, P., Berelson, B. and Gaudet, H. (1944) *The People's Choice*. New York: Columbia University Press.

Lowndes, V. (2002) 'Institutionalism', in D. Marsh and G. Stoker (eds), *Theory and Methods in Political Science* (2nd edn). Houndmills: Palgrave Macmillan.

Case Studies

case studies

9

Case studies can provide for an engaged exploration of a research project or scenario as it develops in a *real-world setting*. They are described by Moses and Knutsen (2007: 132) as 'histories with a point'. Without stating the obvious, a case study is a detailed look at a single political unit/model (an actor, system or structure). The subject is often a bounded one, the focus being on a particular place, time, group or the like. In brief, the subject being used as the study is relatively easy to identify. Examples are single-country studies, a political party or a defined political process. It is important to note that, at the outset, the case study does not compare two or more countries, parties or processes.

This said, the relationship between case study research and comparative research is an important one – case studies frequently form the basis of comparative analysis, with large-*n* comparative studies employing limited data. By contrast, true case studies are characterized by detail and depth.

The purpose of the case study can be threefold (see Lijphart's (1971) case study typology). First, to act as an illustration in its own right – we have a genuine interest in an event or phenomenon. Second, we may be interested in a political unit that can provide an example of a larger body of political actors, parties or processes in order to test an existing hypothesis or theory. The case study does not, however, automatically lead to the output lending itself to generalizations. For example, a case study of Canadian foreign policy during the 1980s does not lead to a generalized understanding of Canadian foreign policy over time, nor does the case study imply a better understanding of the foreign policy of other states. Third, is the hypothesis-generating case study (Lijphart cited in Moses and Knutsen, 2007) – a precursor to the second type, in which the case study generates a theory or hypothesis. Simply put, the case study is a study of a particular example and not a sampling study where the researcher has 'removed' a unit or model from a larger group in order to say something about the whole community. Although the case study is focused on an example, it allows for a development of knowledge that may be derived from the findings of the study and tested by other researchers on other examples. An example of **hypothesis testing** can be seen in Hooghe's (2005: 861) case study of the European Commission, in which she develops 'theoretical expectations about how time, organizational structure, alternative processes of preference formation, and national socialization affect international socialization'.

There is no single way to conduct a case study and, as a result, a combination of research methods can be used. Classical case studies depend on ethnographic and participant–observer methods. They are mostly descriptive examinations, usually of a small number of events or settings (such as local councils, community action groups, development projects) where the researcher is immersed in the topic and uses a variety of **qualitative methods** to analyse both the individual case study and also most often a 'cross-case' result. As a cautionary note in this regard, the researcher must be aware that doing even relatively modest, illustrative case studies is a complex task that cannot be accomplished through occasional, brief investigations. The demands with regard to design, data collection and reporting can be, and often are, substantial.

When multiple cases are used, the researcher may often provide a detailed account of each and then some form of cross-case comparison (summarized in narrative or table formats). More times than not, multiple cases are preferred to single cases, particularly when the cases may not be a complete representation of the population or when varied experiences, situations or behaviours are desirable. However, when including multiple cases the researcher has to be aware of the limits to the depth in which each case can be analysed and this has implications for the structure and length of the research project. When evaluating the data for multiple cases, where each case, for example, may represent a different thematic finding or situation, such as a different political party, country or stance on the environment, the researcher can cluster the results together or discuss each of the cases in terms of running themes across them, to varying degrees.

Methods often employed in case studies are context, **sampling** and data analysis. The context provides the background and contemporary information about the case, including the relevant biographical and social information (depending on the researcher's focus), such as the political setting, the data collection site(s) or other relevant descriptive information associated with the case and situation. Purposeful sampling is generally used in case study research, thus explaining the sampling procedures and the selection of case(s) and the defining characteristics and uniqueness of the case. The researcher has to be aware that careful sampling is crucial because attrition can affect longitudinal case studies that are based on just one or two participants or situations. Turning to the question of data selection, the researcher can draw from either one primary source (such as journals, oral interviews, government reports) or multiple sources. As in much research, bringing together more than one method and perspective (**triangulation**) often leads to added texture and greater insight in analysis. This can enhance the **validity** of the research results. Observations and data sets may range from the natural to the artificial, from the structured to the unstructured, depending on the purpose of the research project. In Hooghe's case, she used surveys that incorporated both semistructured personal interviews and structured attitudinal questionnaires.

Case study data analysis generally involves proceeding from the general to the more specific – for example, beginning informally during the interview or observation stage and continuing until the development of recurring themes or patterns that lead to categories of issues becoming evident in the course of the research. When written records are available, the coding of data and the subsequent analysis can draw the researcher to identify the salient points and, hence, the outcomes of the case study. Having additional coders is usually important when looking into the analyses of texts, interactive patterns (such as between voters and parties or voting patterns on particular issues), as well as discourse, although this is commoner in quantitative research than it is in qualitative research.

What becomes important in all these scenarios is the interpretation that is pulled out from the cases. By establishing the significance or importance of the findings, the researcher should link them to a larger theoretical or practical issue. Leaving the case studies as generalizations is not the point of the exercise. The data may be analysed and interpreted from the position of a variety of ideological standpoints (**feminism**, critical theory, poststructuralism and so on) although the descriptive approach is also common.

FURTHER READING

Lijjphart, A. (1971) 'Comparative politics and the comparative method', *American Political Science Review*, 65 (3): 682–93.

Morse, J.M. (ed.) (1994) *Critical Issues in Qualitative Research Methods*. London: Sage.

Moses, J.W. and Knutsen, T.L. (2007) *Ways of Knowing: Competing methodologies in social and political research*. Houndmills, Basingstoke: Palgrave Macmillan.

Patton, M.Q. (1990) *Qualitative Evaluation and Research Methods* (2nd edn). London: Sage.

Yin, R.K. (1989) *Case Study Research: Design and method*. Newbury Park, CA: Sage.

EXAMPLES

Gerring, J. (2004) 'What is a case study and what is it good for?', *American Political Science Review*, 98 (2): 341–54.

Hooghe, L. (2005) 'Several roads lead to international norms, but few via international socialization: A case study of the European Commission', *International Organization*, 59 (4): 861–98.

Woods, M. (1998) 'Researching rural conflicts: Hunting, local politics and actor-networks', *Journal of Rural Studies*, 14 (3): 321–40.

key research concepts in politics & international relations

Causality and Correlations

It is often the case in political research that we are looking for relationships between **variables**. By this we mean that we want to go beyond demonstrating what happens in the world (for example, that election turnout is on the decline, human rights operate at different levels in different countries) and explain why this occurs. This is particularly important to those concerned with normative questions, as being able to explain why traditions or policies may succeed or fail is integral to establishing 'a better world'.

It is important that we are clear about the difference between causality (which implies a level of predictive power between the independent and dependent variables) and correlation (which implies an association between variables but not necessarily a relationship of causality). For example, we might find that retired people are more likely to vote in an election than those in their early twenties – this is a correlation. We can only claim that causality exists if they vote *because* they are older. In fact, they may vote because they have more time to do so or because the issues that are being debated (provisions for pensioners, investment in care for the elderly) are more relevant to those who are retired than those who are much younger. It is the other factors associated with age that are influential, not age itself.

The main 'challenge', so to speak, for political researchers is that relationships between variables are not as visible as they may be for researchers of the natural world. Think, for example, of the effect of heat on water – we can turn on a kettle and observe steam emerging as the water heats up. Much of what we are interested in as political researchers is not directly observable, so has to be measured by means of surveys, interviews and textual analysis. If we were to stand outside a polling station on polling day and ask electors how they intended to vote, we might observe that older people tend to respond 'Conservative', but there are many 'hidden' variables and they may be more influential on their voting than (perceived) age.

As researchers we need to be confident about *time order*. By this, we mean that we need to be sure the cause preceded the effect. This may be relatively straightforward in an experimental situation – we can place people in a laboratory environment and introduce various stimuli to assess whether or not behaviour is affected (as displayed in Stanley Milgram's now infamous psychological experiments on conformity – see Margetts and Stoker, 2010). However, experimental research of this nature is rare in political analysis and, when asking people to respond to a survey, they may not have entirely accurate memories of the order in which events occurred (this is especially the case when we are asking people to recall events that happened in the past). In their study of media effects on voting behaviour, Norris et al. (1999) emphasize the fact that cross-sectional surveys (such as the British Election Study) can highlight associations between media use and political attitudes but do not in themselves explain the direction of causality. In an attempt to address this issue, Sanders and Norris (Norris et al., 1999) conducted an experiment to measure the effect of news coverage on voter perceptions in 1997, focusing on the potential influence of particular messages, speeches or events. By exposing a sample of a little over 1000 participants to a 30-minute video compilation of television news, Sanders and Norris found some limited evidence that positive news improved the strength of preference for both the Labour and Conservative parties.

One way to test quantitatively for relationships between **variables** is through regression analysis and multiple regression analysis. Tests of correlation include the chi squared test, Spearman's coefficient and Pearson's coefficient and, indeed, all statistical tests of correlation produce results that can show whether or not three kinds of relationships exist. These are that there is no correlation, there is a positive correlation (a change in direction of one variable is matched by a change in the same direction of the other variable) or a negative correlation (a change in direction of one variable is matched by a change in the opposite direction of the other variable).

While political researchers frequently make claims about the strength of various correlations, being confident that these represent causality is more of a challenge. First, the laws of social science are not as predictable as those of the natural sciences – societies, political structures and actors change over time and so do the outcomes of their actions. Second, political actions and phenomena are influenced and constrained by a range of complex and interrelated variables. To assume that a change in just one, easily quantifiable variable is the only cause of change in the dependent variable is perhaps naive (as illustrated by the example of older voters being pro-Conservative).

We could, in principle, test for relations between an almost infinite range of variables. This would not, however, be sensible and we must not make the mistake of identifying *untheorized correlations* (Burnham et al., 2004: 140). If there is a lack of theoretical justification for the relationship to exist, then establishing a correlation makes little sense. We may find, for example, that political corruption is more prolific in countries with hot climates than cold ones, but a claim of corruption being linked to the average daily temperature lacks a theoretical grounding. Problems with explanation also can arise if we identify a *spurious correlation* – that is, we identify a relationship between the independent and dependent variables when, in fact, a third variable is important. The older voters may vote Conservative not because of their age, but because they tend to live in areas with high levels of antisocial behaviour and believe that the Conservative party offers the best policy for dealing with this. If the older residents were replaced by younger ones, they would be likely to make the same voting choice, regardless of age.

As King et al. (1994: 79) state:

> no matter how perfect the research design, no matter how much data we collect, no matter how perceptive the observers, no matter how diligent the research assistants, and no matter how much experimental control we have, we will never know a causal inference for certain.

This important distinction is highlighted in Putnam's work on civic engagement and social capital. His detailed study of Americans indicates a correlation between civic disengagement and the amount of television watched. A policymaker may take this information to argue that television viewing should be monitored to discourage the growth of politically disengaged couch potatoes, but Putnam (2000: 235) warns that the time order relationship may have been misunderstood and it may be the case that:

> People who are social isolates to begin with gravitate toward the tube as the line of leisurely least resistance. Without truly experimental evidence ... we cannot be sure that television itself is the *cause* of disengagement.

Voting behaviour is clearly one area of political research that has generated much debate about causality and correlations – why do voters choose one party and not others? Some (brave) researchers engage in election forecasting, utilizing time series data derived from opinion polls to predict how parties will perform. A good example is Sanders' (2005) study using popularity function models that he claims have been relatively accurate since 1992. In order to explain popularity function, Sanders identifies a number of possible explanatory factors, including objective economic performance, subjective perceptions about the state of the economy, perceptions about economic management competence, perceptions of the party leaders, government reputation for honesty and trustworthiness, evaluations of public service delivery, the costs of ruling and events. By conducting ordinary least squares regression analysis, Sanders (2005: 187) is able to make a series of predictions, but quite cautiously warns, 'Election forecasting, in my view, is more of an art than a science. It involves using what we know about past relationships between variables to make informed guesses about what is likely to happen in the future.'

FURTHER READING

Bryman, A. and Cramer, D. (1994) *Quantitative Data Analysis for Social Scientists*. Abingdon: Routledge. pp.7–15.

King, G., Keohane, R.O. and Verba, S. (1994) *Designing Social Enquiry*. Princeton, NJ: Princeton University Press. pp. 76–91.

Margetts, H. and Stoker, G. (2010) 'The experimental method: Prospects for laboratory and field studies', in D. Marsh and G. Stoker (eds), *Theory and Methods in Political Science* (3rd edn). Houndmills, Basingstoke: Palgrave Macmillan.

Pennings, P., Keman, H. and Kleinnijenhuis, J. (1999) *Doing Research in Political Science*. London: Sage. Chapter 6.

EXAMPLES

The British Journal of Politics and International Relations, 7 (2) (2005), special edition on election forecasting. This provides some good examples of causal analysis.

Burnham, P., Gilland, K., Grant, W. and Layton-Henry, Z. (2004) *Research Methods in Politics*. Houndmills, Basingstoke: Palgrave Macmillan.

Norris, P., Curtice, J., Sanders, D., Scammell, M. and Semetko, H.A. (1999) *On Message*. London: Sage.

Putnam, R.D. (2000) *Bowling Alone*. New York: Touchstone.

Sanders, D. (2005) 'Popularity function forecasts for the 2005 UK General Election', *The British Journal of Politics and International Relations*, 7 (2): 174–90.

Comparative Method

Comparative research is extremely commonplace in international political research. It is not restricted to the subfield of comparative politics, although, obviously, it is traditionally found there. The comparative method is highly applicable in other fields because it is 'a broad-gauge, general method, not a narrow, specialized technique' (Lijphart, 1971: 683). It helps to identify aspects of social and political life that are general across units (that is, institutions, nations, states, regions, cultures), as opposed to being limited to one unit alone. All political researchers want to generalize to some degree. For example, positivist researchers are interested in discovering general laws or patterns of political participation that hold across societies. Hague and Harrop (2007) give four reasons for the need to compare:

- It enables the contextualization of knowledge. If we base all theories on one case, we may be subject to ethnocentric claims that are the exception to the norm rather than the norm itself.
- It can improve classifications (such as what are the common characteristics of authoritarian regimes?)
- It enables us to devise and test hypotheses (such as do particular electoral systems inhibit the election of female candidates?)
- It enables us to make predictions (such as will governing parties lose elections if they preside over a period of economic instability?).

Kohn (1987), in his analysis of cross-national research, discussed four types of comparative research: cross-national, transnational, case study comparative and cultural context research. In cross-national studies, he identifies four further subtypes, these being:

- object – typical here would be comparisons that focus on understanding particular countries because the country is of interest, rather than a hypothesis requiring tests and the country happening to be a convenient case
- context – here it is the phenomenon that is of interest, while the countries being studied are merely the vehicles for comparison (Kohn cites Skocpol's studies of revolution as a good example of this)

- unit of analysis – such studies focus on the way in which political institutions and processes are related to variations in national characteristics
- transnational – here we are often interested in politico-economic systems, such as capitalism or developing nations.

Central to the quality of comparative analysis is the process of case selection (Burnham et al., 2004: 58). This centres on two criteria:

- How many (or how few) comparisons to make – the larger the number of cases we have to compare, the more likely we are to move into the sphere of quantitative analysis (as was the case with Rusciano's (2003) study). It should be noted that a single case may be studied, which seems rather odd at first glance. Such a study, however, facilitates 'thick description' – that is, there is only one case, so the researcher can look at a range of variables. Such idiographic studies often concentrate on the historical dimension of the unit. Many of them focus on the European Union as some researchers view it as sui generis.
- The features of research design – here we can refer to two approaches, which are most similar research designs (MSRD), also known as 'the method of agreement', and most different research designs (MDRD), also known as 'the method of difference'.

A MSRD compares 'two or more cases that are as different as possible in terms of the *independent variable(s)* and as similar as possible on all the spurious and intervening variables', while a MDRD compares 'two or more cases that are as similar as possible in terms of the *independent variable(s)* and as different as possible on all the spurious and intervening variables' (Burnham et al., 2004: 63, italics added). Landman (2005: 555) highlights this approach in the small-*n* comparison study of human rights. Inglehart and Norris (2003: 20) favour a MDRD in their analysis of gender equality and cultural change. They acknowledge that the desire to 'distinguish systematic clusters of characteristics associated with different dimensions of gender equality' leads to trade-offs in which the contextual depth to be gained from a small-*n* study is inevitably sacrificed. In contrast, the MDRD approach enables them to analyse the shift in basic values across different political economies, differing religions and political systems with differing democratic traditions.

To ensure that we know which method to adopt, consideration needs to be given to *what* we want to compare. Researchers must be rigorous when defining the phenomena to be compared or their findings may have reduced **validity**. Researchers must be alert to the 'travelling problem' – that is, when the meaning of **concepts** may alter in different spatial and temporal contexts. De Lombaerde et al. (2010) acknowledge such conceptual pluralism as an issue for consideration in comparative regional studies.

Comparative analysis is not without its critics. For example, 'MacIntyre doubts the entire project of a comparative political science' in relation to theoretical explanation via cross-cultural and law-like causal generalizations (Moses and Knutsen, 2007: 222). In relation to Almond and Verba's (1963) well-known research on civic culture, MacIntyre questions the extent to which 'pride' is a comparable concept – with the same value in different cultures. For MacIntyre, there are specific political features that do not lend themselves to comparison because we cannot separate them from the environment in which they are created – political attitudes derive from the political institutions and practices to which they relate and *cannot* be identified separately.

A second challenge is the appropriate identification of all possible independent, intervening and spurious **variables**. This is illustrated by Rusciano's (2003: 361) study of national identity across 23 nations which highlighted the 'complex relationship among factors of national-focused and international-focused perspectives, all of which combine in the negotiation of national identity'. The interaction between these national and international characteristics is not a uniform one – they vary according to national characteristics. Just as with 'pride', we find the ability to compare is limited.

If we were to compare the political economic status of women in different political systems, we might find that different cultures place different types of emphasis on particular occupations and careers. For example, in some states, certain high-status occupations may be male-dominated, while, in others, concerted attempts may have been made to mainstream gender, particularly in areas such as engineering and medicine. Hopkin (2002) draws attention to the **reliability** of large-n quantitative comparative studies that use per capita gross domestic product (GDP) as a measure of economic success. Different countries may experience different levels of formal and informal economies and, as it is an official statistic generated by governments, it is subject to the usual criticisms that **official data** is subject to (see **secondary analysis**). 'Small n, many variables' studies, too, are criticized on the grounds that the plethora of variables allied to the narrow terrain of the study makes it very difficult to extrapolate any firm findings concerning the variables

comparative method

under consideration and, obviously, to comment sensibly on the generaliz-ability of any findings. That said, the 'small-n' approach has its advocates and much recent work has been done in the field of democratic transition and consolidation using **qualitative methods** within this approach.

FURTHER READING

Burnham, P., Gilland, K., Grant, W. and Layton-Henry, Z. (2004) *Research Methods in Politics*. Houndmills, Basingstoke: Palgrave Macmillan. Chapter 3.

Hague, R. and Harrop, M. (2007) *Comparative Government and Politics: An introduction* (7th edn). Houndmills, Basingstoke: Palgrave Macmillan.

Hopkin, J. (2002) 'Comparative methods', in D. Marsh and G. Stoker (eds), *Theory and Methods in Political Science* (2nd edn). Houndmills, Basingstoke: Palgrave Macmillan.

Inglehart, R. and Norris, P. (2003) *Rising Tide: Gender equality and cultural change around the world*. Cambridge: Cambridge University Press.

Landman, T. (2003) *Issues and Methods in Comparative Politics: An introduction* (2nd edn). Abingdon: Routledge.

Lijjphart, A. (1971) 'Comparative politics and the comparative method', *American Political Science Review*, 65(3): 682–93.

MacIntyre, A. (1972) 'Is a science of comparative politics possible?', in P. Laslett, W.G. Runciman and Q. Skinner (eds), *Philosophy, Politics and Society* (4th series). Oxford: Basil Blackwell.

Moses, J.W. and Knutsen, T.L. (2007) *Ways of Knowing: Competing methodologies in social and political research*. Houndmills, Basingstoke: Palgrave Macmillan.

Peters, B.G. (1998) *Comparative Politics: Theory and methods*. Houndmills, Basingstoke: Palgrave Macmillan.

Ragin, C.C. (1992) *The Comparative Method*. Berkeley, CA: University of California Press.

EXAMPLES

Almond, G. and Verba, S. (1963) *The Civic Culture*. Princeton, NJ: Princeton University Press.

De Lombaerde, P., Söderbaum, F., Van Langenhove, L. and Baert, F. (2010) 'The problem of comparison in comparative regionalism', *Review of International Studies*, 36 (3): 731–53.

Kohn, M.L. (1987) 'Cross-national research as an analytic strategy', *American Sociological Review*, 52 (6): 713–31.

Kopecký, P. and Mudde, C. (2000) 'What has Eastern Europe taught us about the democratisation literature (and vice versa)?', *European Journal of Political Research*, 37 (4): 517–39.

Roberts, A. (2009) *The Quality of Democracy in Eastern Europe: Public preferences and policy reforms*. Cambridge: Cambridge University Press.

Rusciano, F.L. (2003) 'The construction of national identity: A 23-nation study', *Political Research Quarterly*, 56 (3): 361–6.

Concepts

Concepts are the building blocks of social science research. Such concepts are more than mere labels as they are 'more or less abstract representations of the social world' (della Porta and Keating, 2008: 2). They constitute attempts by researchers to translate the complex and multifaceted phenomena they encounter into units that can be subjected to measurement and evaluation. Concepts, then, are a fundamental part of the thinking process, allowing researchers to represent their observations, reflect on them, develop theories, conduct debates and so, hopefully, build on our understanding of the world. Concepts allow researchers to distil the complexities of the social and political world into manageable pieces. This is a particularly challenging task for political researchers as the world of politics is 'broadly defined and fluid, characterised by "grey" areas, and reflexivity is a key component in analysis' (Savigny and Marsden, 2011: 18). Given this context, concept formation is not a straightforward process.

Concepts may be accepted as an essential part of the grammar of politics, but not everyone speaks the same language. The labels assigned to concepts may mean different things to different people. Like much else in political research, then, concepts are contested. Indeed, some concepts are 'essentially contested', which means that not only do people disagree about their meaning but also there is no hope of any consensual understanding because the different interpretations are competitive rather than complementary (Gallie, 1955).

Some such contested concepts arise because, over time, their labels have become stretched. We can see this clearly in the use of labels such as 'governance' and 'Europeanization', for example. Concepts are picked up in academic discourses and moulded or reinterpreted to fit with the particular theoretical approaches of the researchers. Thus, 'governance' may be and is applied in a relatively narrow way, referring to the making/evolution of rules, norms and principles outside the sphere of formal government. Governance thus is seen as complementary to government. Other approaches, though, view 'government' as subsumed within the wider practices and processes of governance. In this view, government is but one actor in a pluralistic, polyarchic arena – and, indeed, arguably one of the less influential actors. Olsen (2002: 923–6) identifies five different definitions of 'Europeanization': geographical extension of Europe, especially in terms of EU membership; a European level of governance, including but not restricted to the agency of the EU; the influence of European-level actors, rules and norms on national and subnational levels of governance; the spread of European institutions, norms and values beyond the region of Europe; and as an agenda for greater political union within Europe.

Essentially, contested concepts, such as 'power', 'justice', 'rights' or 'good', are value-laden as they do more than simply describe the observed – that is, 'what is' – they suggest what 'ought' to be. The usage of such labels is infused with subjective, normative leanings. How the researcher defines and operationalizes such concepts reflects their own ontological, epistemological and ideological assumptions and such researchers compete 'to establish a particular conception of a concept as objectively correct, as in the case of "true" democracy, "true" freedom, "true" justice and so forth' (Heywood, 2000: 7). Researchers may strive to be neutral, but their internal bias may well affect their formation and use of normative concepts in particular.

Concepts are affected, too, by the vagaries of fashion and fad in research. Some are most definitely 'in', while others are most definitely 'out', dependent on the prevailing trajectories of research programmes. This fluctuation can be seen when we read about researchers 'bringing the State back in' or effecting 'the return of culture'.

The inclusion of the concept of 'culture' has ebbed and flowed in political research. Early interpretations were restrictive, seeing 'culture' as representative of 'national character' and using it in efforts to explain why different people acted or reacted differently in different places. This usage is evident in Almond and Verba's early work on political culture, *The Civic Culture*. Their findings and conclusions were contested on both methodological grounds – using individual-level surveys to extrapolate society-level findings – and because of their underpinning assumptions – that American values were 'superior' and had global resonance.

As rational choice approaches rose in prominence within political research, so culture ebbed. There was little room for this concept in approaches that emphasized the individual as a rational, decision-making unit. Culture latterly reappeared with the 'constructivist turn' in politics and international relations as issues concerning identity and intersubjective understandings especially became more salient. The context and climate of academic research then affects the conceptual currency in use.

Political research, fundamentally, is all about comparison. Concepts, notwithstanding contestation, allow us to try to identify what we see in our research and evaluate our observations. It is vital, then, that, at the start of our research process, our conceptualization is clear and concise: 'the first task of any researcher is to specify the nature of the objects of their research, and hence to define the primary concepts with which she is concerned' (Mair, 2008: 179). Our research will be only as useful as our conceptualization allows it to be. 'Flabby' concepts that lack focus and finesse will be less than helpful. We need to make sure that we are comparing the comparable. Sartori's (1970: 1038) 'ladder of abstraction' highlights the need for reflective thinking on what to compare:

> Classes are required to be mutually exclusive, i.e., class concepts represent characteristics which the object under consideration must either have or lack. Two items being compared must belong first to the same class, and either have or have not an attribute; and only if they have it, the two items can be matched in terms of which has it *more* or *less*.

As the definition of the concept moves up the ladder, it is extended, accommodating additional attributes. The higher up the ladder, the more 'stretched' the concept and the more decreased its analytical precision. On the upper rungs of the ladder, the concepts are increasingly abstract and more heterogeneous in terms of their characteristics, so little benefit can accrue from comparison. As this occurs, we run the risk of undermining the **inferences** to be drawn from empirical research. On the bottom rungs, though, comparison may well be too restricted, so any findings are limited in their applicability and/or their contribution to theorization. In the middle, then, we find the most productive area for research, as Mair (2008: 188) notes:

> where the concepts have a medium extension [that is, range of cases] and a medium intension [that is, number of characteristics] and can travel across a reasonably wide range of cases, theory-building and analysis in the social sciences is often at its most interesting and challenging.

Sartori's hierarchical taxonomy to aid effective comparison can be seen in Lijphart's (1968) typology of democratic systems. Different democratic systems are presented and ordered with reference to two key variables: societal structure and elite behaviour. This ordering facilitates comparison and the extrapolation of reasons for there being different kinds of regimes: 'consociational democracies differ from centrifugal democracies *because* of the different pattern of elite behaviour' (Mair, 2008: 183). Interest in comparative research on democracies was stimulated further by democratization processes after the Cold War. Research in this area progressed as different constellations of attributes led to new conceptualisations of democracy and a plethora of labels such as 'restricted democracy', 'illiberal democracy' and, 'oligarchical democracy' (Collier and Levitsky, 1997).

Concepts are essential to political research. We need to be clear and reflexive in their formation and usage. Concepts help us to simplify the complexities of the political world, but they always remain constructs – manufactured representations of perceptions of 'reality'. As such, we need to bear in mind that they are not 'value-free' and even the most apparently simple labels may be more than they seem: 'Words have meanings, some even have multiple meanings and some have contested meanings. When conceptualizing, you should therefore remember to explicate and specify the meaning of the concepts you have decided to employ' (Jørgensen, 2010: 221).

FURTHER READING

della Porta, D. and Keating, M. (2008) 'Introduction', in D. della Porta and M. Keating (eds), *Approaches and Methodologies in the Social Sciences: A pluralist perspective*. Cambridge: Cambridge University Press. pp. 1–15.

Gallie, W.B. (1955) 'Essentially contested concepts', *Proceedings of the Aristotelian Society*, 56: 167–98.

Heywood, A. (2000) *Key Concepts in Politics*. Houndmills, Basingstoke: Palgrave Macmillan.

Jørgensen, K.E. (2010) *International Relations Theory: A new introduction*. Houndmills, Basingstoke; Palgrave Macmillan.

Mair, P. (2008) 'Concepts and concept formation', in D. della Porta and M. Keating (eds), *Approaches and Methodologies in the Social Sciences: A pluralist perspective* Cambridge: Cambridge University Press. pp. 177–97.

Sartori, G. (1970) 'Concept misinformation in comparative politics', *American Political Science Review*, 64 (4): 1033–53.

Savigny, H. and Marsden, L. (2011) *Doing Political Science and International Relations: Theories in action*. Houndmills, Basingstoke: Palgrave Macmillan.

key research concepts in politics & international relations

EXAMPLES

Almond, G.A. and Verba, S. (1963) *The Civic Culture*. Princeton, N.J.: Princeton University Press.

Almond, G.A. and Verba, S. (1980) *The Civic Culture Revisited*. Boston, MA: Little, Brown.

Collier, D. and Levitsky, S. (1997) 'Democracy with adjectives: Conceptual innovation in comparative research', *World Politics*, 49 (3): 430–51.

Lijphart, A. (1968) 'Typologies of democratic systems', *Comparative Political Studies*, 1 (1): 3–44.

Lukes, S. (2005) *Power: A Radical View* (2nd edn). Houndmills, Basingstoke: Palgrave Macmillan.

Olsen, J. (2002) 'The many faces of Europeanisation', *Journal of Common Market Studies*, 40 (5): 921–52.

·············· Content Analysis ··············

Much of the research we conduct within politics and international relations involves the examination and interpretation of text, images and speeches. As a student, you are by now familiar with reading books, articles and newspapers and summarizing and comparing arguments and evidence in order to fulfil assessment requirements. From a *methodological* perspective, we need to do this in a systematic and organized manner. Two dominant approaches are utilized to achieve this in our disciplines: content analysis and **discourse analysis**.

Holsti (1969: 14) defined content analysis as 'any technique for making inferences by objectively and systematically identifying specified characteristics of messages'. Content analysis is a well-established qualitative research method and was especially popular during the Cold War era when Sovietologists pored over Soviet domestic and international communications trying to decode and uncover the meaning and intent therein.

Content analysis is used to determine the significance of an issue by measuring and examining the salience that it is given in communications – by whom is the issue raised, in what context is it raised, how often and where is it raised and so on. This method can help trace the trajectory of issues as they make it on to a policy agenda, for example, and can help

content analysis

to demonstrate how such issues gain 'traction'. Content analysis also can be used to identify and quantify bias in reporting in the press and on television – as with the well-known work of the Glasgow University Media Group. In one of its research projects, it analysed both textual and visual coverage of industrial unrest. It demonstrated bias in the coverage, with managers depicted as reasonable and progressive in stark contrast to entrenched and implacable strikers (Glasgow University Media Group, 1976).

Content analysis can be used to examine not only manifest content but also latent content. In the latter focus, the researcher categorises the language used as well as developing categories for the ideas and **concepts** that they believe are embodied within the language and structure of the sources. In latent content analysis, then, the researcher 'shifts the focus to the meaning underlying the elements on the surface of a message' (Potter and Levine-Donnerstein, 1999: 259).

As with other research methods, how to 'do' content analysis will be determined by the research question of the project. The issue of **sampling** needs to be decided at the outset. If the topic to be covered relates to a specific event – such as the verbal and non-verbal language used by candidates in televised general election debates – then the temporal scope of the sample is set. Other topics, however, may not be so contained and the researcher needs to set the parameters of the study. If the study wanted to identify and explain trends in media coverage of groups opposed to the war in Iraq, for example, then the researcher would need to decide which time period to focus on, which type(s) of media to include and which days/times during the week's coverage are to be examined. Generally, probability sampling will be used, with researchers choosing a day of the week at random to look at the output from the sources and then to visit the source on every 'n^{th}' day for the agreed period of the study.

When researchers know what it is that they wish to examine, then they need to narrow down what it is they wish to count. These units of analysis may take the form of the key players – that is, when the issue is raised, who puts it forward? If it is in the written press, who wrote the article? Where does it appear within the newspaper, how many column inches does it get? If it is in a party manifesto, is it given special mention? How many paragraphs does it get? Does the coverage attract the eye or is it hidden away on the page? These matters need to be addressed to aid the production of a coding schedule and a coding manual for the project.

The schedule is the form on which each coder will record the data found on the topic. If the topic was, for example, press coverage of the war in Afghanistan, researchers may want to record the title of the newspaper that had the story, the date and relevant page of the issue, the headline of the story, the category of the story (politics, economics, environment), the type of story (opinion piece, editorial, feature piece, news item), the location of the story on the page (lead story, for example), the length of the story, if it had photographs with it and so on. These data would help identify the manifest content of the story – as would the recording of the keywords used within the story.

A more focused content analysis would also study the latent content of the story – looking at the implicit understandings and messages within the story, underneath and between the words of the text. The coding schedule then would allow for the recording and categorization of all this data prior to its analysis. A coding manual or code book is produced as the common guide allowing each coder on the project to see the different categories into which to allocate their specific findings – it reminds them of what they are looking for and how to code it once they find it. This manual should be devised collectively so that the coders have the opportunity to discuss, agree and so 'own' the categories. During the data-gathering phase, the coding team should meet regularly so that they can agree and make any refinements to the manual. These discussions can help to enhance intercoder **reliability** and, consequently, reinforce the **validity** of the research findings. All the coders also need to check that they are consistent over time in their identification and categorization of data. Random checks using their own earlier coded sources will help them to ensure intracoder reliability. The coding manual means that the different coders all use the same rules for the systematic interpretation of the data. The research findings then should be replicable by other researchers using the same rules on the same sources.

Content analysis can prove an overwhelming task on the surface. Researchers narrow the potential sources of data by deciding to sample that which is available, then have the coding manual and schedule to further contain the data and render it manageable. Content analysis has benefited from developments in information technology in the form of computer-assisted qualitative data analysis (CAQDAS). Such software programmes as ATLAS.ti, NVivo and Transana (for audio/video sources) reduce the intensive workload associated with content analysis by assisting with the organization and management of data. Ultimately, however, researchers have to guard against becoming too dependent on the technology and letting it do the thinking and theorizing for them.

Content analysis is a highly transparent research method that allows for the analysis of a wide range of text and non-text sources. While measures can be taken to help maximize inter- and intracoder reliability, subjectivity cannot be eradicated completely. This research method does depend on human interpretation – ultimately, individuals decide what to code and how to code it. Advocates of content analysis, however, would not see such interpretation as a drawback of this method, but, rather, a core strength, as quantitative, statistical approaches may well miss nuanced, latent meanings within the sources. A more valid criticism of content analysis as a research method is its relative weakness in answering the 'Why?' question. It can demonstrate how an issue is covered and analyse that coverage, but it is less good at explaining why the issue became the subject of attention in the first place.

FURTHER READING

Glasgow University Media Group (1976) *Bad News*. London: Routledge & Kegan Paul.
Holsti, O.R. (1969) *Content Analysis for the Social Sciences and Humanities*, Reading, MA: Addison-Wesley.
Payne, G. and Payne, J. (2004) *Key Concepts in Research Methods*. London: Sage.
Potter, W. and Levine-Donnerstein, D. (1999) 'Rethinking validity and reliability in content analysis', *Journal of Applied Communication Research*, 27 (3): 258–84.

EXAMPLES

Dimitrova, D.V. and Connolly-Ahern, C. (2007) 'A tale of two wars: Framing analysis of online news sites in coalition countries and the Arab world during the Iraq War', *Howard Journal of Communications*, 18 (2): 153–68.
Druckman, J.N., Jacobs, L.R. and Ostermeier, E. (2004) 'Candidate strategies to prime issues and image', *The Journal of Politics*, 66 (4): 1180–202.
Murray, C., Parry, K., Robinson, P. and Goddard P. (2008) 'Reporting dissent in wartime: British press, the anti-war movement and the 2003 Iraq War', *European Journal of Communication*, 23 (1): 7–27.

Deduction/Induction

The process of generalizing from what we have observed to what we have not or cannot observe is called induction. It forms the basis of scientific theory... Deductive reasoning moves from abstract statements about general relationships to concrete statements about specific behaviors. (Manheim et al., 2008: 19–20)

There are two approaches we can take towards conducting research. We can start with a research **hypothesis** – for example, 'policies that reduce the national deficit will influence voting behaviour at the next General Election'. To address such a statement, we would gather evidence (such as opinion poll trends, political party documents, political speeches) in order to support or refute the hypothesis. This is a process of deduction (much like Sherlock Holmes or Miss Marple would use to solve a crime). However, we do not always begin research with such a well-defined statement. Rather, we may decide to explore an event or phenomenon (for example, a sudden increase in the number of political representatives from a previously under-represented social group), gather data and then develop a relevant hypothesis – this is an inductive approach.

The debate between inductivists and deductivists is one of those 'What comes first?' scenarios: the general or the particular? Deductivists opt for the former, while the inductivists opt for the latter. Deductivists infer from the general to their particular case and inductivists infer from the particular to the general. This debate about approaches reflects their differences in terms of **epistemology** and **ontology**. Deductivists are positivist and objectivist in these matters, while inductivists are interpretivist and constructionist.

Using a deductivist approach, researchers will become immersed in the theoretical knowledge base already existing in the field of study. They use this knowledge base to deduce a hypothesis. They then collect and analyse their data and subsequently use their findings to confirm or invalidate their hypothesis. Their specific findings then lead to a revision of the theories and/or models in the field of study. We can see that there is a linear push in this research trajectory (on paper at least). The deductive approach is common in political research – not least because students often are steered towards it by their supervisors. This approach is favoured by quantitative researchers and can be clearly seen in rational choice studies of political phenomena (Marsh and Furlong, 2002: 36–7).

In contrast to deduction, induction starts with the particular case(s). Theory is not the starting point but the destination for this research trajectory. Inductive researchers primarily are theory-builders rather than theory-testers. They tend to favour qualitative approaches – in keeping with their understanding of political actors, factors and relationships as situated 'within a cultural perspective, where culture denotes a web of shared meaning and values … [so] Theory is important but it is not always established prior to the research as in the deductive-empirical approach' (della Porta and Keating, 2008: 26–7).

Researchers using an inductive process start off with the topic, generate a hypothesis and collect the data. They then analyse the data and from this analysis comes the theoretical explanation of the phenomenon under observation. Such researchers have few preconceptions at the start of the research process. Rather, the concepts and theory emerge from the data-collection and analysis phases. Inductive logic can be seen in the work of multi-level governance theories (Marsh and Furlong, 2002: 36–7).

Grounded theory is strongly associated with the inductive approach – deriving from the work of anthropologists and ethnographers. It is a term that rarely appears in political science methods texts. The principles of grounded theory have been developed through the work of Glaser and Strauss since the 1960s (Harrison, 2001: 78). Rather than testing a hypothesis, the grounded approach is one in which theories (or explanatory frameworks) 'emerge' as the research data is collected. The advantage is that there is no preconceived idea of what is important or meaningful, but, rather, more realistic theories develop as data is collected. Concepts can be refined and are subject to regular retesting. 'Grounded theories, because they are drawn from data, are likely to offer insight, enhance understanding, and provide a meaningful guide to action' (Strauss and Corbin, 1998: 12). For example, Brown (1999) examines the role that regime theory plays in understanding urban politics and explores the hitherto underexplored areas of governance and public–private arrangements. In doing so, he employs a grounded theory methodology to explore AIDS politics in the New Zealand city of Christchurch. He justifies this method by arguing that regime theory is itself not 'testable' because it contains internal inconsistencies. As such, a grounded theory approach is most appropriate when the aim is to 'generate more useful social theory' (Brown, 1999: 77).

In theory (or, more accurately, regarding the role of theory), we can distinguish between deductive and inductive research strategies, but, in practice, it is hard to do so. Abduction relates to the iteration between deductive and inductive processes. Researchers often traverse between the two strategies – identifying and generating hypotheses from the existing theoretical knowledge base, but then refining and adapting such theories and models during the data-collection phase, then deriving their specific research findings to add to the knowledge base. This iterative process 'involves a weaving back and forth between data and theory' (Bryman, 2001: 10) and is becoming more common in political research programmes.

FURTHER READING

Bryant, A. and Charmaz, K. (eds) (2007) *The SAGE Handbook of Grounded Theory.* London: Sage.

Bryman, A. (2001) *Social Research Methods.* Oxford: Oxford University Press.

della Porta, D. and Keating M. (2008) 'How many approaches in the social sciences?: An epistemological introduction', in D. della Porta and M. Keating (eds), *Approaches and Methodologies in the Social Sciences.* Cambridge: Cambridge University Press. pp. 19–39.

Harrison, L. (2001) *Political Research: An introduction.* Abingdon: Routledge.

Manheim, J.B., Rich, R.C., Willnat, L. and Brians, C.L. (2008) *Empirical Political Analysis* (7th edn). Harlow: Pearson.

Marsh, D. and Furlong, P. (2002) 'A skin, not a sweater: Ontology and epistemology in political science', in D. Marsh and G. Stoker (eds), *Theory and Methods in Political Science* (2nd edn). Houndmills, Basingstoke: Palgrave Macmillan. pp. 17–41.

Strauss, A. and Corbin, J. (1998) *Basics of Qualitative Research* (2nd edn). London: Sage.

EXAMPLES

Brown, M. (1999) 'Reconceptualizing public and private in urban regime theory: Governance in AIDS politics', *International Journal of Urban and Regional Research*, 23 (1): 45–69.

Friedrichs, J. and Kratochwil, F. (2009) 'On acting and knowing: How pragmatism can advance international relations research and methodology', *International Organization*, 63 (4): 701–31 (on abduction).

Henderson, E.A. (2009) 'Disturbing the peace: African warfare, political inversion and the universality of the democratic peace thesis', *British Journal of Political Science*, 39 (1): 25–58 (on deduction).

Zürn, M. and Checkel, J.T. (2005) 'Getting socialized to build bridges: Constructivism and rationalism, Europe and the nation-state', *International Organization*, 59 (4): 1045–79 (on induction).

deduction/induction

While **content analysis** is associated with both **quantitative** and **qualitative methods**, the same is not the case for discourse analysis – these approaches (and there are several of them) lie clearly within *qualitative* methods. The emphasis here is not so much on the number of times a word or phrase is used but on the meaning that is attached to such words and phrases.

The 'constructivist turn' in politics and International Relations research facilitated an increased interest in this research method, but it already was well-established in other disciplines such as media studies, policy analysis and social psychology.

Discourse analysis focuses on communication as an active dimension of the social world. Researchers using such approaches analyse the language of political actors to reveal what it says about the actors' perceptions of the world and their roles in it. Language is not seen solely as a medium of communication; rather, it represents and is affected by cultural and social institutions and structures. Discourse, in the Foucauldian sense, refers to a system of representation in which there is a link between language and practice (what is often referred to as social action).

Conversational analysis focuses on 'naturalistic' language – in particular, the way in which certain institutions and organizations develop a vocabulary. Rather than seeing language as purely a means of (political) communication, the emphasis is on the *dynamic* nature of discourse – it not only reflects the political world but is also actually constitutive of social relations. Language is both socially influenced and socially constitutive. It is a way of 'doing' as much as a way of saying – a way to legitimize some views and ideas and delegitimize others.

Discourses are ways of representing and categorizing 'reality' and peddlers of competing discourses try to sell their versions of reality above all others. The more resonant often are the more simplistic, as Burnham et al. (2008: 250) observe: 'These discourses may often be organized in terms of binary opposites contrasting, for example, the First and Third Worlds; good and evil; development and underdevelopment; and democracy and authoritarianism'. Such Manichean discourses are found in relation to George W. Bush's case for the 'war on terror' – 'a war between good and evil', 'between freedom and fear' (Kellner, 2007: 626).

When certain discourses become embedded, they are hegemonic, having crowded out contending interpretations of the events or issues concerned. They have triumphed by selling their own 'truth' and dismissing the claims of other 'illegitimate' accounts. Krebs and Lobasz (2007), for example, explore how the 'meaning' of 9/11 was fixed, by the Bush Administration within the context of the 'war on terror', thereby delegitimizing and suppressing other counter-narratives as dissent and un-American. The Bush Administration was, they argue, able to sell a discourse of the 9/11 events that suited its wider foreign policy objectives. The events themselves were packaged and interpreted to this end: 'September 11, like all political events, did not speak for itself. It required interpretation, and it did not have to lead to a War on Terror. It mattered how it was publicly represented and by whom, how and whether those representations were contested' (Krebs and Lobasz, 2007: 413).

A further illustration is provided by Fairclough's (2000) examination of the language of New Labour. In doing so, he highlights the prominent role played by non-elected advisors (such as Alistair Campbell) in centralizing the entirety of the Party's message – making political communication inseparable from the process of policymaking itself. In particular, Fairclough focuses on New Labour's discourse surrounding social welfare and welfare reform.

Clearly there are important factors that influence discourse – for example, culture and social change. In terms of the data sources commonly engaged with by discourse analysts, these include transcripts of speeches, reports, interviews and images (including cartoons and political graffiti), as well as political pamphlets. As with content analysis, discourse analysis involves coding in order to organize and manage the material to locate common themes, patterns and categories. Specifically, the focus is on latent content, which then will be situated within the wider social and cultural world.

Traditionally, discourse analysts have been more critical of the effective use of coding software (such as CAQDAS) than many content analysts, on the grounds that such programs cannot identify and convey the covert and constitutive meanings of language. Unsurprisingly, discourse analysts are critical of terms such as **reliability** and **validity**, viewing them as positivist criteria that are inappropriate to their field of study.

discourse analysis

FURTHER READING

Burnham, P., Gilland Lutz, K., Grant, W. and Layton-Henry, Z. (2008) *Research Methods in Politics* (2nd edn). Houndmills, Basingstoke: Palgrave Macmillan.
Gee, J.P. (2005) *An Introduction to Discourse Analysis*. London: Routledge.
Laclau, E. and Mouffe, C. (1985) *Hegemony and Socialist Strategy*. London: Verso.
Phillips, L. and Jørgensen, M.W. (2002) *Discourse Analysis as Theory and Method*. London: Sage.

EXAMPLES

Fairclough, N. (2000) *New Labour New Language?* Abingdon: Routledge.

Kellner, D. (2007) 'Bushspeak and the politics of lying: Presidential rhetoric in the "War on Terror"', *Presidential Studies Quarterly*, 37 (4): 622–44.

Krebs, R.R. and Lobasz, J.K. (2007) 'Fixing the meaning of 9/11: Hegemony, coercion, and the road to war in Iraq', *Security Studies*, 16 (3): 409–51.

Lazar, A. and Lazar, M.M. (2008) 'Discourse of global governance: American hegemony in the post-Cold War era', *Journal of Language and Politics*, 7 (2): 228–46.

Documentary Analysis

Political research inevitably relies heavily on documentary sources – we easily reach for books, journal articles and newspapers and official reports in order to secure the information we need to address research questions. We may develop this with primary, archived sources, such as private papers, memoranda and notes. However, we probably give less thought to the process by which we *analyse* such documents – that is, the framework by which we systematically examine such sources. Indeed, documentary analysis can focus on two aspects (and may encompass both) – that is, first, what is being 'said' or 'shown' and, second, the context in which such documents were actually created. Taking this second consideration first, it would make little sense to evaluate all documents in the same way.

Documents differ in relation to *type* (such as government records, the mass media and personal sources), *intended audience* (produced for open access/mass circulation, targeted at a specific audience, such as an internal memo, or written with a very limited circulation in mind, such as private correspondence) and *institutional/legal limitations to access* (such as the 1958 Public Records Act – there is a 30-year release delay on many government documents in the UK, for example). Furthermore, selection bias (Vromen, 2010) is subject to not only what documents *are* available but also by our *awareness* of what exists. These concerns are common to what is referred to as historiography – an approach often adopted by those concerned with institutionalism and the explanation of political events and processes via the context in which they occur (Vromen, 2010). In contrast, an interpretivist approach to documentary analysis is more likely to engage with **discourse analysis**.

In taking a step back from 'what is on the page' (or, more commonly, in the recording), we should pay attention to what we might describe as the 'political' aspects of archival research. For example, Burnham et al. (2004: 169) draw attention to the issue of what *counts* as acceptable material for analysis and suggest that Politics and International Relations 'retains by and large a "top-down" methodological focus, in which the principal, secondary and tertiary material remains published diaries, memoirs, letters, biographies and parliamentary papers and debates'. This applies especially to the creation and support of archives. Some examples include the Churchill Archives, Margaret Thatcher Foundation, Nixon Presidential Materials and the Golda Meir Collection, 1904–1987. Miles (1989) is one of many to highlight the marginalization of the role of women in history. Indeed, '[w]hat people decide to record is itself informed by decisions which, in turn, relate to the social, political and economic environments of which they are a part' (May, 1997: 164). 'The main limitation of such data is the tendency to produce "top-down" studies … in my experience, archival analysis alone cannot bridge the gulf and must therefore be supplemented wherever possible with oral histories and interview techniques' (Vickers, 1995: 176).

A challenge that is put to documentary analysis is that it is a 'reactive' process – we can only examine what is there to be examined, it cannot react to our probing. Scott (1990) highlights four particular areas for concern when dealing with such material:

- authenticity – soundness and certainty about authorship (such as the Hitler diaries, Zinoviev letter)
- credibility – similarity and accuracy: 'the extent to which the evidence is undistorted and sincere, free from error and evasion' (Scott, 1990: 7)
- representativeness – survival and availability (typicality, mood at the time)
- meaning – literal and interpretative understanding (use of codes in personal documents).

Finally, we should be wary of confusing quantity with quality: 'The sheer range and diversity of documentary sources can appear bewildering to the inexperienced researcher' (Burnham et al., 2004: 165).

FURTHER READING

Burnham, P., Gilland, K., Grant, W. and Layton-Henry, Z. (2004) *Research Methods in Politics*. Houndmills, Basingstoke: Palgrave Macmillan.

May, T. (1997) *Social Research: Issues, methods and process* (2nd edn). Buckingham: Open University Press.

Miles, R. (1989) *The Women's History of the World*. London: Paladin.

Scott, J. (1990) *A Matter of Record*. Cambridge: Polity Press.

Vickers, R. (1995) 'Using archives in political research', in P. Burnham (ed.), *Surviving the Research Process in Politics*. London: Pinter.

Vromen, A. (2010) 'Debating methods: Rediscovering qualitative approaches', in D. Marsh and G. Stoker (eds), *Theory and Methods in Political Science* (3rd edn). Houndmills, Basingstoke: Palgrave Macmillan.

EXAMPLES

Autesserre, S. (2009) 'Hobbes and the Congo: Frames, local violence, and international intervention', *International Organization*, 63(2): 249–80.

Bicchi, F. (2011) 'The EU as a community of practice: Foreign policy communications in the COREU network', *Journal of European Public Policy*, 18 (8): 1115–32.

Carrapatoso, A. (2011) 'Climate policy diffusion: Interregional dialogue in China-EU relations', *Global Change, Peace & Security*, 23 (2): 177–94.

Flinders, M. (2009) 'Conserving the Constitution: The Conservative Party and democratic renewal', *The Political Quarterly*, 80 (2): 248–58.

Johansson, K.M. (2002) 'Party elites in multilevel Europe: The Christian Democrats and the Single European Act', *Party Politics*, 8 (4): 423–39.

Newman, J. (2010) 'Towards a pedagogical state? Summoning the "empowered" citizen', *Citizenship Studies*, 14 (6): 711–23.

.... Ecological Fallacy ....

Political researchers frequently are involved in trying to establish cause and effect (see **causality and correlations**). Research has demonstrated, for example, that particular sociodemographic characteristics may enhance political participation or revolutions are underpinned by structural influences. However, just because two changes appear to occur at the same time does not mean that they are related. Clarity in relation to the definitions and categories that researchers employ is vital, and changes in any one of these can present a different aggregate picture. A debate among those working with large quantitative data sets is that claims are incorrect – not because the researcher has falsified information, but because what appear to be trends at an aggregate level are not evident if we revert to the micro-level data: 'The ecological fallacy refers to instances in which inappropriate **inferences** about relationships at the individual level are made on the basis of aggregate data obtained at the area level' (Pantazis and Gordon, 1999: 201).

This is not to imply that researchers intentionally mislead. Ecological fallacy may occur because we do not have access to the most detailed level of data. Schatz sought to accurately explain the breakdown of democracy and rise of fascism in the Spanish Second Republic (1931–6). The 'challenge' that Schatz (2001: 160) faced was that

> Unfortunately, no individual-level data on socio-economic position, voting behaviour or party membership are available for the period of the Spanish Second Republic. Analyses must be based on aggregate electoral results, party membership rolls, censuses and government records gathered at the provincial level.

Several studies reinforce this concern with **validity**. First, Inglehart (1988) has used data from a range of countries to suggest that national political culture is an important indicator of stable democracy, as interpersonal trust generates pro-democratic values and leads to democracy in operation. The flaw in this claim, according to Seligson (2002), is that this relationship may be subject to ecological fallacy. By using additional sources of data, Seligson points to shortfalls in Inglehart's conclusions. When revisiting relationships at the micro-level, Seligson found that those in the survey who indicate a high degree of interpersonal trust are not necessarily those who demonstrate democratic attitudes or behaviour.

Second, Garner et al. (1988) revisited claims that had been made about unemployment among school-leavers in Scottish cities. Their concern was many studies supporting the 'characteristics approach' were based on aggregate data that considered boroughs and areas rather than individuals. The implication from the characteristics approach is that 'personal characteristics are found to dominate the chances of a given individual being unemployed' (1988: 133) – that is, the individuals need to change in order to become employable. By reverting to an analysis of individual-level data, Garner et al. (1988: 143) were able to reinforce the validity of the characteristics approach, with the added qualification that 'the effects of living in a disadvantaged area appear through a lower level of attainment in school-leaving examinations and hence impact on the school leaver's chances of employment' – education becomes a mediating variable rather than the sole explanatory variable.

Third, in attempting to shed light on differing levels of political participation over time and space, Lister (2007) rejects the appropriateness of individual-level data, instead favouring pooled cross-section time series analysis of aggregate data. As a result, a methodological debate ensued between Arzheimer and Lister via the pages of the *British Journal of Politics and International Relations*, in which Lister (2009: 518) recognized that there are 'limitations of quantitative methods to provide solid and robust evidence to certain questions'. In response, Arzheimer maintains correlating aggregate **variables** that are interpreted as indicators of individual agency constitute an ecological fallacy.

Finally, Hobolt and Wittrock (2011) interrogate the validity of the second-order election model that is often tested at aggregate data level (the model has cross-national credence in demonstrating that the lesser importance of second-order elections is exhibited in lower levels of turnout, greater support for smaller parties and the so-called 'punishment' of governing parties). By utilizing an experimental approach (which limits the external validity of the research – that is, can the results be used to predict voter behaviour in a genuine election?), Hobolt and Wittrock generate an individual-level model of voter choice. Rather than undermining the second-order voting thesis, Hobolt and Wittrock reinforce the claims made regarding sincere and strategic second-order voting and as such concerns about a possible ecological fallacy being generated are dismissed.

Hence, the opportunity for research to generate ecological fallacies is an important issue when considering the employment of large-scale data sets. We can compare levels of data to an onion – just as the flavour might intensify as we discard outer layers in favour of those closer to the centre, we might also find that the picture presented alters as we move from the macro level (such as country or region) to the micro (such as community or individual cases). Macro-level analysis can produce misleading trends and we research in an environment in which micro-level data is not necessarily easily accessible to all.

FURTHER READING

Inglehart, R. (1988) 'The renaissance of political culture', *American Political Science Review*, 82 (December): 1203–30.

Pantazis, C. and Gordon, D. (1999) 'Are crime and fear of crime more likely to be experienced by the "poor"?', in D. Dorling and S. Simpson (eds), *Statistics in Society*. London: Arnold.

Seligson, M.A. (2002) 'The renaissance of political culture or the renaissance of the ecological fallacy?', *Comparative Politics*, 34 (3): 273–92.

EXAMPLES

Arzheimer, K. (2009) 'Lakatos reloaded: A reply to Lister', *British Journal of Politics and International Relations*, 11 (3): 526–8.

Garner, C., Main, B. and Raffe, D. (1988) 'The distribution of school-leaver unemployment within Scottish Cities', *Urban Studies*, 25: 133–44.

Hobolt, S.B. and Wittrock, J. (2011) 'The second-order election model revisited: An experimental test of vote choices in European Parliament elections', *Electoral Studies*, 30 (1): 29–40.

Lister, M. (2007) 'Institutions, inequality and social norms: Explaining variations in participation', *British Journal of Politics and International Relations*, 9 (1): 20–35.

Lister, M. (2009) 'Methods, theories and evidence: A reply to Arzheimer', *British Journal of Politics and International Relations*, 11 (3): 518–25.

Schatz, S. (2001) 'Democracy's breakdown and the rise of fascism: The case of the Spanish Second Republic, 1931–6', *Social History*, 26 (2): 145–65.

Empirical Analysis

empirical analysis

39

Political researchers often label themselves as being primarily driven by descriptive studies (empiricists) or prescriptive debates (theorists or normative analysts) although, in reality, much research combines both approaches, with an emphasis on one or other strand. Empirical political theory involves the testing of statements against what happens in the real world (Monroe, 1997). Empirical analysis focuses on explaining what happens, but also may try to explain why (see **causality and correlations**).

A clear example of the significance of empirical analysis is the emergence and dominance of the behavioural school of political analysis and **behaviouralism**. Assisted by the introduction of appropriate **methods** in the form of large-scale surveys, the behavioural school originated in the USA in the 1920s before being pursued in the UK from the 1950s onwards and is concerned with trends in political behaviour and activity. Empirical analysis is central to the development of **rational choice** theory.

Empirical analysis can be traced back to a philosophical theory of knowledge known as **positivism**, which is associated with the work of John Locke. The emphasis is on that which exists in the world and is independent from researchers and their values, which enables us to test statements (often in the form of a **hypothesis**), provide explanations and, where appropriate, make predictions. Empirical analysis forms the basis of inductive approaches to political analysis. As Sanders (2002: 63) states, 'if an explanation is to be believed, it must make empirically falsifiable predictions that can be tested against observation.'

A strength, and appeal, of empirical analysis is that it can map trends over time. For example, are trends in electoral turnouts stable or is there evidence of a long-term decline? The evidence from empirical analysis can help set agendas for political reform and inform policymaking. Knowledge about trends in political participation can help us to make statements about the extent to which a country is democratic. Political parties take note of public opinion trends if they want to win elections. International alliances are formed and broken on the basis of political actions and personal negotiations.

However, the idea that everything in politics is 'measurable' is misleading and there are many political questions to which empirical analysis cannot provide an adequate answer. As Hopkin (2002: 254) states, 'Empirical reality is instead rather messy and political scientists can only limit, rather than eliminate, extraneous variance through careful research design.' The contentious nature of this 'empirical reality' is demonstrated by the 'Hawthorne effect', which is that those being studied modify their behaviour because they know they are being studied. Recognition of this effect has itself led to an important re-evaluation of the role of psychological experimentation in social science with a shift towards a preference for ethnographic observational and in-depth interview research (Payne and Payne, 2004: 107–11).

Another concern is how much empirical evidence we need in order to justify or refute a claim or prediction. Empirical political scientists are constantly engaged in a process of retesting and refining theories based on new evidence (see **case studies** and **comparative method** for more discussion). An example of this is when Cowley and Garry (1998) employed an empirical analysis of voting behaviour in the second ballot of the 1990 UK Conservative leadership contest. They focused on testing seven hypotheses of voting behaviour that relate to socio-economic, political and ideological variables in order to explain why John Major became party leader and prime minister. By using data on voting intentions gathered from published lists of MPs' declarations, interviews with each of the leadership campaign teams and correspondence with MPs, they were able to argue with confidence that educational background, parliamentary experience and, most importantly, attitudes to Europe were the key factors determining the voting choices of MPs. In particular, they (1998: 494) stressed the importance of explanatory refinement:

> We knew from an earlier study that by the end of the 1987 Parliament the EU question had emerged as the most potent ideological division within the party, eclipsing divisions over economics and morality, which were previously seen as the key underlying divisions within the party.

The multivariate analysis conducted on the 1990 contest revealed a number of influential variables (social class, parliamentary experience and attitudes towards Europe) and a number of non-influential variables (age, constituency marginality, occupation).

Duch and Strøm (2004) test, both theoretically and empirically, the argument that political values in advanced democracies have changed significantly, with the Right and Left having realigned along new value dimensions. They in particular challenge the view (as supported by Kitschelt) that political conflict in mature democracies is increasingly organized around a Right–authoritarian versus Left–libertarian dimension. Empirical testing of survey data from the Euro-Barometer and World Values Surveys leads them to claim that empirical studies often have been insufficiently attentive to different forms of authoritarianism and the results of earlier studies 'may, therefore, have been biased' (2004: 258).

Bieler and Morton (2004) employed empirical analysis to assess the activities and joint strategies of labour and social movements at the first European Social Forum (ESF) held in Florence in 2002, with particular reference to their resistance to both neoliberalism and its extra-economic enforcement through military power, as evidenced by the war on Iraq. Bieler and Morton adopted an 'observer-as-participant' methodology, relying on direct observations and interviews without intensive participation in the events observed. Validation of the data gained at the ESF was

empirical analysis

achieved through cross-checking with written primary material by trade unions and social movements, either collected directly at the ESF or obtained from these groups' Internet sites, as well as follow-up interviews with representatives of established trade unions, new trade unions and social movements.

FURTHER READING

Hay, C. (2002) *Political Analysis: A critical introduction*. Houndmills, Basingstoke: Palgrave Macmillan. pp. 78–80, 252–3.

Monroe, K.R. (1997) *Contemporary Empirical Political Theory*. Berkeley, CA: University of California Press.

Payne, G. and Payne, J. (2004) *Key Concepts in Research Methods*. London: Sage.

Sanders, D. (2002) 'Behaviouralism', in D. Marsh and G. Stoker (eds), *Theory and Methods in Political Science* (2nd edn). Houndmills, Basingstoke: Palgrave Macmillan.

EXAMPLES

Bieler, A. and Morton, A.D. (2004) '"Another Europe is possible"?: Labour and social movements at the European social forum', *Globalizations*, 1 (2): 305–27.

Cowley, P. and Garry, J. (1998) 'The British Conservative Party and Europe: The choosing of John Major', *British Journal of Political Science*, 28 (3): 473–99.

Cunningham, D.E., Gleditsch, K.S. and Salehyan, I. (2009) 'It takes two: A dyadic analysis of civil war duration and outcome', *Journal of Conflict Resolution*, 53 (4): 570–97.

Duch, R.M. and Strøm, K. (2004) 'Liberty, authority, and the new politics: A reconsideration', *Journal of Theoretical Politics*, 16 (3): 233–62.

Finke, D. (2009) 'Challenges to intergovernmentalism: An empirical analysis of EU treaty negotiations since Maastricht', *West European Politics*, 32 (3): 466–95.

Hopkin, J. (2002) 'Comparative methods', in D. Marsh and G. Stoker (eds), *Theory and Methods in Political Science* (2nd edn). Houndmills, Basingstoke: Palgrave Macmillan.

Epistemology

Political and international relations research is not, and cannot be, judgement-free and, as such, there are certain standards by which we define and judge what we are studying. It is precisely because political researchers adopt differing ontological and epistemological standpoints that we are faced with so many explanations of the same phenomenon.

Epistemology is the branch of philosophy that studies the theory of knowledge (Grix, 2002: 177). Essentially, it is the attempt to understand what is *real* knowledge and what is *false* knowledge. How do we know what we know is true? Marsh and Furlong (2002: 17) say epistemology (and **ontology**) is like a skin rather than a sweater, meaning that 'most often those positions are implicit rather than explicit, but regardless of whether they are acknowledged, they shape the approach to theory and the methods which the social scientist utilises.' That is, we cannot 'take off' or change our epistemological position: it is impressed within us and influences our view of what is valid as an area of study.

Epistemology focuses on what we know and how we can know it, so 'what you see depends on where you stand'. How rich and poor, men and women, old and young, black and white, understand the world is likely to differ. An epistemological stance rests on a claim that is justified as being 'truthful' and of value to the research, hence the notion of politics as a *science*. Here, then, we focus on what we can classify as 'real' or 'objective', what is true knowledge. We hope, if not expect, that when carrying out an investigation, researchers are as objective and value-free as possible. That is to say, researchers analyse what really happens rather than pick and choose cases that reinforce their own beliefs. Thus, social and political researchers consent to follow certain agreed procedures when conducting research and their epistemological position will influence the **methods** they employ. Practically, then, researchers must see their approach to an investigation of the political as a scientific **methodology**, asking 'How can I as a researcher develop theories or models that are better than competing theories?'

When looking at the history of epistemology, we can see a clear trend, in spite of the confusion of many seemingly contradictory positions. The first theories of knowledge stressed its absolute permanent character (what we now refer to as **positivism**), whereas the later theories, those mainly utilized in political research, put the emphasis on its relativity or situation-dependence, its continuous development or evolution and its active interference with the world and its subjects and objects (what we refer to as relativism and postmodernism). The whole trend moves from a static, passive view of knowledge towards a more adaptive and active one as 'Knowledge, and the ways of discovering it, is not static, but forever changing' (Grix, 2002: 177).

epistemology

In his exploration of comparative politics, Landman (2000) establishes the epistemological basis on which his own research is grounded. He recognizes that studies of comparative politics straddle the extremes – that is, for some, knowledge has an absolute permanent character while, for others, it is relative and culturally bound. Landman (2000: 16) positions himself 'somewhere in between', saying there are certain deductive theories that can be tested in the real world, although knowledge cannot be 'value-free'. Brunskell (1998: 41) suggests that feminist epistemological concerns can be understood via an exploration of the feminist critique of mainstream social research, which, prior to the 1970s, privileged 'a prior belief that biological differences between men and women constituted the *natural* basis upon which the different *social* relations between men and women were organized.' This 'knowledge' – men and women are different – constituted the basis of the assumption that men, as social beings, formed the public sphere of politics, while women were marginalized to the private sphere of politics. 'The result was that social researchers found it impossible to understand fully women's experiences' Brunskell (1998: 41), hence producing an andocentric understanding of the political world. This can have an impact on **methodology** and the outcomes of research.

Furthermore, we can identify 'trends' in terms of how particular phenomena are analysed. Theories regarding the nature of conflict, for example, are constantly being revised as the perceived purpose of war changes in emphasis (witness the general move away from interstate territorial conflict towards substate conflict over religious and ethnic autonomy) and the process of conflict develops (the ground battles of the world pre-1945 have been largely replaced by technological, notably aerial, warfare).

Patomäki (2001) traces the epistemological developments of positivism and critical theory in peace research from the 1930s onwards and suggests that the 'end of the Cold War' posed a challenge to both the ontology and epistemology of peace research. Patomäki suggests one area of 'knowledge' in peace research that may need to be revisited is the relationship between politics and violence.

Both Grix (2002) and Hay (2002) provide a useful model to represent the role of epistemology in political research. The process begins with **ontology** (what we think is out there to know), the second stage is epistemology (what and how we can know about it), the third stage is **methodology** (how can we go about acquiring the knowledge), the fourth stage is **methods** (which tools do we apply to gain the knowledge) and the final stage is sources (what data can we collect). The process of political research should be carried out in that order – we do not start with a preferred method or methodology and work backwards to establish our epistemological standpoint. What we tend to see as a result of these stages in the research agenda process is that positivist-inclined researchers predominantly engage with **quantitative methodologies**, while interpretivist-inclined researchers predominantly engage with **qualitative methodologies**. Note, we place an emphasis on *trends* and *tendencies* – to assume that there is no overlap of the various applications of methodological approaches is neither true nor appropriate.

FURTHER READING

Grix, J. (2002) 'Introducing students to the generic terminology of social research', *Politics*, 22 (3): 175–86.

Hay, C. (2002) *Political Analysis*. Houndmills, Basingstoke: Palgrave Macmillan.

Marsh, D. and Furlong, P. (2002) 'A skin, not a sweater: Ontology and epistemology in political science', in D. Marsh and G. Stoker (eds), *Theory and Methods in Political Science* (2nd edn). Houndmills, Basingstoke: Palgrave Macmillan.

EXAMPLES

Brunskell, H. (1998) 'Feminist methodology', in C. Seale (ed.), *Researching Society and Culture*. London: Sage.

Keating, M. (2009) 'Putting European political science back together again', *European Political Science Review*, (1) 2: 297–316.

Landman, T. (2000) *Issues and Methods in Comparative Politics: An introduction*. Abingdon: Routledge. pp. 15–16.

McAnulla, S. (2007) 'New Labour, old epistemology?: Reflections on political science, new institutionalism and the Blair government', *Parliamentary Affairs*, 60 (2): 313–31.

Maynard, M. (2002) 'Studying age, "race" and gender: Translating a research proposal into a project', *International Journal of Social Research Methodology*, 5 (1): 31–40.

Patomäki, H. (2001) 'The challenge of critical theories: Peace research at the start of the new century', *Journal of Peace Research*, 38 (6): 723–37.

Smith, M.J. (2008) 'Re-centring British Government: Beliefs, traditions and dilemmas in political science', *Political Studies Review*, 6 (2): 143–54. (Provides a useful critique of Bevir and Marsh's interpretivist approach to British governance.)

epistemology

Ethics are intrinsic to the conduct of good research and should never be viewed as an optional 'extra' for research projects. Whether you are the principal investigator in a research programme with a huge budget or a first-year undergraduate writing an essay, doing research ethically is crucial.

What, then, are 'ethics'? 'Ethical principles distinguish socially acceptable behaviour from that which is considered socially unethical' (Moule and Hek, 2011: 35). Transposed to the field of research, this means that the gathering, handling, storing and use of research findings must be conducted in an ethical manner.

The two main approaches to ethics are duty-based ethics/deontological ethics and results-based ethics/consequentialism. The former approach is associated with the work of Immanuel Kant and is a principle-based view of ethics – we ought to do the right thing because it is intrinsically the right thing to do and must avoid doing the wrong thing because it is intrinsically the wrong thing to do. We cannot justify our action on the grounds that it later produced good ends – our duty is to do the right thing even if it yields bad results. Kant argued even that it would be wrong to tell a lie in order to prevent a friend's murder. Instead, there always was and is a duty to tell the truth (Kant, 1797/1949). This categorical imperative to tell the truth in all circumstances and regardless of the consequences reflects the universalist reading of ethics that underpins this stance. Applied to research, this duty-based approach means that 'Research ethics take on a universal form and are intended to be followed regardless of the place and circumstances in which the researcher finds themselves' (May, 1997: 55).

The results-based/consequentialist approach to ethics focuses on the results of an action rather than the action itself. Our actions should be governed by consideration of their consequences. This approach is commonly related to the work of John Stuart Mill (1863). An action is ethical if its results are more beneficial than harmful. The more benefits that derive from an action, the more ethical the action is: 'Actions are right in proportion as they tend to promote happiness, wrong as they tend to produce the reverse of happiness. By happiness is intended

key research concepts in
politics & international relations

pleasure, and the absence of pain; by unhappiness, pain and the privation of pleasure' (Mill, 1863: Chapter 2).

Duty-based/deontological ethics with their stress on universal moral rules seem a rather tall order for many researchers. Such absolutism would be very hard to realize in practice, as Burnham et al. (2008: 284) point out: 'In terms of an injunction to avoid deception, it is rather utopian. Should researchers be held to higher standards of behaviour than the population at large?' Results-based/consequentialist ethics, too, however, pose challenges when putting them into practice. Instead of a universalist approach that never changes and to which each case must be assigned, here we have an approach where every decision has to be evaluated as sui generis. Researchers would need to be able to foretell the consequences of their actions so they could judge whether their behaviour would prove ethical or not. This seems a very costly approach in terms of time and effort. There is the danger, too, that, if the ends are seen to justify the means, then potentially an 'anything goes' approach could emerge with all sorts of dangers along the way. No one disputes the need for ethical behaviour in research, but clearly there are contending views on what it is.

Principles to guide the ethical conduct of research have been codified to help guide researchers in their work. Such attempts at codification emerged in the wake of World War II following the Nazi biomedical experimentation on human subjects. The Nuremberg Code (1947) and the Declaration of Helsinki (1964) are key international documents that provide guidelines to govern research based on 'the fundamental principle that *the ends do not justify the means in the pursuit of knowledge*' (Denscombe, 2010: 331). They embed core research principles that, in turn, have influenced regional, national and local codes of conduct and professional guidelines. The essence of ethical and, thus, good research is that the researchers do not cause harm. The obvious worth of a stricture to avoid harm, however, may not be as simple to implement as it may at first appear.

'Harm' is a subjective concept and may be interpreted in a variety of ways. This is evidenced by the controversial Milgram experiments. In July 1961, Milgram (1974), a psychologist at Yale University, started an experiment to discover how willing people were to obey authority figures.

Research participants were assigned to the role of 'teacher' and invited/encouraged to give electric shocks to 'learners' who, based in a nearby room, answered set questions incorrectly. In reality, the 'learners'

ethics

were 'in' on the experiment and no electric shocks were actually being given, although the 'learners' acted the part, responding more violently as the 'voltage' increased. Should a 'teacher' have misgivings and want to stop, a researcher would encourage them to continue on the grounds that the experiment demanded their continued participation and the 'learner', while experiencing pain, was not suffering irreparable harm.

In the first round of the experiment, 65 per cent (almost two thirds) of the 'teachers' delivered the most intense shock available – 450 volts – despite their own disquiet. As Milgram (1973: 62) put it, 'Stark authority was pitted against the subjects' moral imperatives against hurting others, and with the subjects' ears ringing with the screams of the victims, authority won more often than not'.

These experiments were controversial due to the ethical concerns raised. The participants were deceived by the researchers – made to believe that they were inflicting pain on others when, in reality, this was not the case. The experiment, too, seemed to lack merit in terms of its external validity – did it really explain why people simply followed orders (the Nuremberg defence) no matter what the cost? Could any such explanatory 'proof' be tested elsewhere in other situations characterized by the mass, systematic violation of human rights (Burnham et al. 2008: 57)?

Ethical guidelines and professional codes of conduct are supposed to help researchers avoid such ethically dubious practice. Researchers should strive to do no harm by observing the core research principles of consent, anonymity and confidentiality.

Participants in research projects should knowingly and willingly consent to their involvement. They should be fully cognisant that their participation is entirely voluntary and they can end it whenever they choose to do so. When researchers approach people to ask them to participate in a project, they need to fully explain the rationale of that project, how the research findings will be collected, how they will be stored and how they will be used. Researchers have a duty to inform the potential participants of any 'harm' that could potentially affect them or their interests due to the project. Such 'harm' may be physical, emotional or reputational. Only when the prospective participants have been so advised are they in a position to give informed consent to their involvement: 'Informed consent is generally taken to mean that those who are researched should have the right to know they are being researched, and that in some sense, they should give their consent'

(Bulmer, 2001: 49). Once participants have consented, they should then be given the name and contact details of the person to contact should they have any further questions about the research.

Anonymity and confidentiality also need to be addressed. Participants should be made aware of how the research data will be stored and assured that their consent is essential for the disclosure of any information pertaining to their involvement. It is important that the anonymity of the participants is protected. Their details should be discussed only by the researchers and then only when it is essential to do so. Researchers also need to ensure that they observe all legal obligations related to prevailing data protection legislation. Once the research has been completed, then any personal data on the participants should be destroyed.

These core research principles appear a matter of 'common sense' in most respects, but their observation in practice may prove particularly challenging in different research contexts. Covert research raises significant ethical issues. 'Undercover' researchers do not inform their subjects of the research and so do not gain their consent. These researchers still need to ensure that they do no harm to the participants and their anonymity is protected. In such cases, then, researchers may offset criticism surrounding the lack of consent.

Action research, too, may raise specific ethical concerns because the researchers and the practitioners are so closely linked. In such research projects, 'it is important to have a clear idea of when and where the action research necessarily steps outside the bounds of collecting information which is purely personal and relating to the practitioners alone' (Denscombe, 2010: 132).

Ethical issues may also arise when dealing with the gatekeepers who control access to the research material. Permission must be sought and obtained before the research can go ahead. Gatekeepers will want assurances that the proposed research and the researchers involved are legitimate. Researchers will have to evidence their research credentials and disclose their research objectives so that the gatekeepers can make an informed judgement on the validity of the project and whether or not it will have any potential costs for the subject. More established researchers tend to have a better record of getting past the gatekeepers, so junior researchers should seek their participation – if only for this purpose. More experienced researchers also tend to be better able to recognize and deal with 'the subtle control techniques that [gatekeepers] may deploy' (Burnham et al., 2008: 294).

ethics

Research governance is a necessary yet contested phenomenon, especially among those researchers who use qualitative research methods, as (Punch, 2000: 281):

> While all social research intrudes to some extent in people's lives, qualitative research often intrudes more. Some qualitative research deals with the most sensitive, intimate and innermost matters in people's lives, and ethical issues inevitably accompany the collection of such information.

The core principles of ethical research – consent, anonymity and confidentiality – have been incorporated into multi-level research governance structures for social research at national and local levels – nationally through the two key frameworks of the Economic and Social Research Council's (ESRC's) *Research Ethics Framework* (2005) and its *Framework for Research Ethics* (2010) and locally through the regulations of various research ethics committees (RECs) in institutions such as universities and the codes of conduct for professional associations. Researchers present their proposals, protocols, consent forms and so on to the RECs concerned for their approval. The RECs consider whether sufficient provisions have been made to ensure that the research projects meet ethical requirements.

This review process is seen by some as the essence of good practice: 'the need to get approval from such ethics committees reinforces the point that a concern with ethics is not an option – it is a fundamental feature of all good research' (Denscombe, 2010: 329). Others, however are more critical. There are concerns that the transmission of research governance structures and practices from the 'hard' science world of biomedicine to the 'soft' world of social science research has been problematic on the grounds of 'fit' (Burr and Reynolds, 2010).

The issue of 'risk' in particular is singled out for comment. No one argues that the harm principle is irrelevant in social science research, but they do argue that it is different because it may prove difficult to gauge 'risk' at the onset of a project. Clearly the 'risk' one associates with biomedical research is of a much different nature than that which may characterize a questionnaire on voting priorities. Others have claimed that the standards set are too standardized and the focus is more on the researcher 'jumping through hoops' to obtain approval rather than stimulating genuine ethical deliberation and judgement. Further, there is disquiet that the governance architecture, especially within universities,

has become part of a wider implicit power struggle over what constitutes knowledge and who/what it is for. The highly prescriptive nature
of the 'new ethical bureaucracies in universities' is not seen as a testimony to their 'objectivity, reliability and justifiability, [but rather as] a
chimera because such schemes invariably mask the hidden operation of
subjective power' (Boden et al., 2009: 727, 734). Academic autonomy
and creativity, some argue, may be stifled by intrusive, one-size-fits-
all research strictures, especially given the heterogeneity of the social
sciences (Stanley and Wise, 2010: 6.6):

> There is not one social science community, with very different approaches
> existing which impact on all aspects of research, differentiating the social
> sciences from each other, differentiating even different paradigms and
> methodologies from others in the same discipline. These particularities
> matter because they relate to fundamental matters of how epistemology and
> ontology are conceived, while the supposed universal competence of RECs
> tends to ignore such particularities to focus on 'generalities' which are not in
> fact general at all.

Notwithstanding such critiques, all researchers need to reflect on the
ethics of their work. Their work must have integrity – the findings must
be presented clearly and impartially and not manipulated to suit sponsor
or marker preferences. Equally, of course, the research must be the work
of its researchers.

Plagiarism commonly is defined as 'using the work of others as if it
were one's own' (Rosamond, 2002: 169). It is a growing problem, especially for universities, not least due to the Internet, as it can make cheating
easier and offers countless outlets for students to purchase assessments.
Plagiarism is never acceptable, but there are gradations of offence
depending on the intent to deceive on the part of the plagiarist. These
range from hapless students who plagiarize as a result of their 'shoddy
scholarship' (most commonly consisting of a laissez-faire attitude to ref-
erencing) to the more devious students who knowingly submit work that
is not their own in the hope that the markers will not notice. Despite the
use of detection software, most commonly Turnitin, Rosamond's (2002:
172) conclusion that 'only a minority of serious plagiarists are discovered' seems sound due to the proliferation of sites to aid the dedicated
plagiarist. So too is his recommendation on how we may work together
to limit plagiarism. Sanctions and legal recourse are blunt mechanisms

and unsuitable in terms of fostering a sense of self-generating, self-sustaining ethical behaviour on the part of researchers. Instead, it is through the transmission of a whole normative framework for ethical research that plagiarism may best be managed: 'the resolution of the problem depends less on the development of coercive instruments to deal with the "crime" than on the development of norms that emerge through reflective pedagogy and processes of academic socialization' (Rosamond, 2002: 167).

FURTHER READING

Bulmer, M. (2001) 'The ethics of social research', in N. Gilbert (ed.), *Researching Social Life*. London: Sage. pp. 45–57.

Burnham, P., Gilland Lutz, K., Grant, W. and Layton-Henry, Z. (2008) *Research Methods in Politics* (2nd edn). Houndmills, Basingstoke: Palgrave Macmillan.

Denscombe, M. (2010) *The Good Research Guide: For small-scale social research projects* (4th edn). Maidenhead: Open University Press/McGraw-Hill.

Kant, I. (1797/1949) 'On a supposed right to lie from altruistic motives', Prussian Academy Volume VIII from I. Kant (ed. and trans. Lewis White Beck), *Critique of Practical Reason and Other Writings in Moral Philosophy*. Chicago, IL: University of Chicago Press.

May, T. (1997) *Social Research: Issues, methods and process* (2nd edn). Buckingham: Open University Press.

Mill, J.S. (1863) *Utilitarianism*. London: Parker, Son & Bourn.

Moule, P. and Hek, G. (2011) *Making Sense of Research: An introduction for health and social care practitioners* (4th edn). London: Sage.

Punch, K.F. (2000) *Developing Effective Research Proposals*. London: Sage.

Rosamond, B. (2002) 'Plagiarism, academic norms and the governance of the profession', *Politics*, 22 (3): 161–74.

Stanley, L. and Wise, S. (2010) 'The ESRC's 2010 framework for research ethics: Fit for research purpose?', *Sociological Research Online*, 15 (4): 12.

EXAMPLES

Boden, R., Epstein, D. and Latimer, J. (2009) 'Accounting for ethos or programmes for conduct?: The brave new world of research ethics committees', *The Sociological Review*, 57 (4): 727–49.

Burr, J. and Reynolds, P. (2010) 'The wrong paradigm?: Social research and the predicates of ethical scrutiny', *Research Ethics*, 6 (4): 128–33.

Milgram, S. (1973) 'The perils of obedience', *Harper's Magazine*, 6 December, pp. 62–77.

Milgram, S. (1974) *Obedience to Authority*. New York: Harper & Row.

Ethnography and Ethnomethodology

It could be argued that the theories, **concepts** and analytical frameworks we work so hard as researchers to develop mean nothing until they are applied to 'the world out there'. Put differently, how can we claim to be able to explain political behaviour and decision-making if we have not engaged in some way with those we wish to understand?

Ethnography firmly sits in the qualitative approach to data collection, though, as a method for conducting political research, it is, perhaps, underutilized within the discipline in comparison, for example, to anthropology, sociology or history. However, when ethnographic methods are put into practice, they can often provide detailed and interesting insight into political parties, institutions and the workings of government.

An obvious benefit of ethnography is it avoids the pitfalls of more 'detached' forms of research, which can be a criticism of large-scale surveys. Rather, in ethnographic research we allow people to talk freely and present their perspectives *in their terms*, adopting an inductive methodological approach. Devine (1995: 137) claims that the positive gains of a qualitative approach within Political Science are often neglected when, indeed, its strengths lie in the fact that it:

> involves the researcher immersing her/himself in the social setting in which s/he is interested, observing people in their usual milieux and participating in their activities.

One particular area of political studies that benefits from an ethnographic approach is when the research subject involves *cultures* – the culture of an institution, party or administration.

Deriving, as an approach, from the Garfinkel/Chicago School of sociology in the 1920s and 1930s (though its legacy can be tracked to Weber's idea of *Verstenhen*), the emphasis in ethnomethodology is placed on the construction and conveyance of meaning (Halfpenny, 1984: 8):

Ethnomethodology is founded on the view that every occurrence within the social world is unique or indexical: that is, every event depends for its sense on the context within which it occurs, where the context is made up of the time, the place and the people involved.

Ethnomethodology is studying the ways social actors (communities, states and so on) make sense of the social and political world around them. This method differs from the other *framing* tools for exploring research possibilities as it starts from the assumption that what we see around us is socially constructed. Actors construct the political and social order in life. Hierarchy and order (society, political processes and social order) are constitutive of experiences and observations that actors cannot help but order into a coherent structure so knowledge may be gained. Ethnomethodologists, following on from those such as Garfinkel, maintain that we organize these social constructions as individuals. When we are confronted with a particular context, for example, we select events and facts and then place them into a pattern (such as one reflecting an historical lineage). Our selection and positioning of the 'facts' are affected by our specific cultural contexts. Once we see this emergent pattern, we use it to order subsequent facts and events so that we can make sense of what is happening in government, society or world politics.

This method seeks to illustrate how social actors use their specific cultural contexts and cultural positioning to make sense of everyday events. Without a doubt, this allows for individuals within a shared culture, community or nation to interpret actions and situations similarly. From this standpoint, ethnomethodologists highlight our reliance on communal and cultural routines by utilizing research strategies that break away from these accepted norms and rules. This can be done, for example, by framing our understandings in a different manner (by examining how Members of Parliament from opposing parties react to one another during Prime Minister's Question Time, for instance).

Ethnomethodology demonstrates that, through the study of the findings of such research projects, we can construct, embed and interpret our political hierarchy and social order. The outcome allows researchers to suggest ways in which the community or state constructs an order to its own social and political reality by making sense of the interactions between its members and the interactions between communities or states.

From the perspective of research validity, emphasizing *cultural relativism* (the means by which a society is constructed and operates – the 'rules' of political behaviour), such as the 'Whitehall Village', serves to avoid the accusation of *ethnocentrism* (cultural bias). Yet, as with qualitative research in general, we can be faced with the challenge of having to explain representativeness and generalizability.

FURTHER READING

Devine, F. (1995) 'Qualitative analysis', in D. Marsh and G. Stoker (eds), *Theory and Methods in Political Science*. London: Macmillan.

Flyvbjerg, B. (2001) *Making Social Science Matter*. Cambridge: Cambridge University Press.

Garfinkel, H. (1984) *Studies into Ethnomethodology*. Cambridge: Polity Press.

Geddes, B. (2003) *Paradigms and Sand Castles*. Ann Arbour, MI: Michigan University Press.

Halfpenny, P. (1984) *Principles of Method*. London: Longman.

Hindmarsh, J. and Llewellyn, N. (eds) (2010) *Organisation, Interaction and Practice: Studies in ethnomethodology and conversation analysis*. Cambridge: Cambridge University Press.

Moses, J. and Knutsen, T.L. (2007) *Ways of Knowing: Competing methodologies in social and political research*. Houndmills, Basingstoke: Palgrave Macmillan. pp. 204–17.

EXAMPLES

Carr, E.H. (2001) *The Twenty Years' Crisis: 1919–1939*. Houndmills, Basingstoke: Palgrave Macmillan.

Fukuyama, F. (1992) *The End of History and the Last Man*. London: Penguin.

Gillespie, M. and O'Loughlin, B. (2009) 'News media, threats and insecurities: an ethnographic approach', *Cambridge Review of International Affairs*, 22 (4): 667–85.

Hobsbawm, E. (1996) *The Age of Extremes*. London: Michael Joseph.

Kornprobst, M. (2012) 'From political judgements to public justifications (and vice versa): how communities generate reasons upon which to act', *European Journal of International Relations*, Prepublished July, 18, 2012. DOI: 10.1177/1354066112439218: 1–35.

Scharff, C.M. (2008) 'Doing class: A discursive and ethnomethodological approach', *Critical Discourse Studies*, (4): 331–43.

Stokoe, E. (2006) 'On ethnomethodology, feminism and the analysis of categorical reference to gender in talk-in-interaction', *The Sociological Review*, 54 (3): 467–94.

Wiener, A. (2009) 'Enacting meaning-in-use: qualitative research on norms and international relations', *Review of International Studies*, 35 (1):175–93.

ethnography and
ethnomethodology

Evidence-based Policy Making (EBPM)

It seems counter-intuitive to argue that policy should not be based on evidence: 'It is difficult to imagine anyone arguing that policy should be based on anything but the best available evidence. The concept of evidence-based policy has an intuitive, commonsense logic' (Marston and Watts, 2003: 144). As ever in social science research, though, it all comes down to a matter of meaning. EBPM is a contested concept and practice.

On reflection, this rather innocuous phrase raises significant normative concerns: 'for instance, how should evidence be collected, what evidence should be used and how should that evidence be used?' (Wells, 2007: 23). Such issues reflect the ontological, epistemological and methodological debates inherent in the social sciences. EBPM is positivist in its orientation, as Clarence (2002: 6) observes: 'Decision makers often prefer quantitative data generated by surveys or the analysis of aggregate data to qualitative methods which can be portrayed as anecdotal'. In EBPM, then, 'what is to count is what can be counted, measured, managed, codified and systematised' (Parsons, 2002: 13).

EBPM originated within medicine and healthcare services where it is known as evidence-based medicine (EBM) or evidence-based practice (EBP). It seeks to systematically retrieve and critically review research findings in order to help clinicians make the most informed decisions in their treatment of patients. It adopts a hierarchical approach towards 'evidence'. The 'gold standard' of EBPM is the randomized control trial (RCT), where participants are randomly allocated to treatment groups, then receive alternative forms of treatment (which may include the use of placebos). The researchers can then make informed, evidenced-based judgements about the effectiveness or efficacy of, for example, the drugs or medical technologies they are testing. The random assignment of the participants to the groups helps to reduce selection bias.

Other methods central to EBPM are meta-analyses of statistical data and systematic reviews of qualitative studies (Cochrane, 1972; see, too, the Cochrane Collaboration at: www.cochrane.org and the Campbell Collaboration at: www.campbellcollaboration.org). Literature reviews

key research concepts in politics & international relations

might seem to be more of a **qualitative method** and so sit oddly in this positivist hierarchy of 'evidence' and 'knowledge'. It is important, then, to clarify what constitutes a *systematic* review.

In social science research, literature reviews traditionally tend to be more serendipitous than systematic and, arguably, rather more descriptive than evaluative. A systematic review is based on a transparent search strategy that clearly establishes the research question to be addressed and explicitly explains the types of searches used (manual, automated, mixed), the types of sources used (websites, journals, conferences, digital libraries, databases, search engines and so on), the time period covered by the review, the criteria for the inclusion and exclusion of primary and other studies and how the quality assessment of the studies is to be made. The findings of the review – built on only those sources judged scientifically sound – are then synthesized and disseminated. These matters are explicitly addressed in a systematic review protocol or plan that guides the research project: 'A protocol is ... a useful tool for promoting transparency, transferability and reliability. It outlines what the reviewer intended to do and makes it possible for the review to be repeated at a later date by others' (Young et al., 2002: 220). This concern with robust, verifiable and replicable findings underlines how the review is to be systematic and 'scientific' in origin and execution rather than interpretivist.

EBPM grew from its origins in medicine and healthcare to spill over into the wider domain of public policy. It was contextualized in the perennial re-flaring of the 'white heat of technology', now manifest in developments in IT, not least the Internet, and an informed, well-educated public who could use the plethora of sources of information at its disposal to demand the 'best' of public service providers. It signalled 'a return to the old time religion: better policy making was policy making predicated on improvements to instrumental rationality' (Parsons, 2002: 3). This revival occurred within a policy-making environment that was instrumentalist and managerialist, characterized by an audit culture and a preoccupation with 'value for money'. It was also a time when there had been an erosion of the deferential culture of trust in public officials, such as teachers, doctors and police officers, and, consequently, 'an increasingly educated, informed and questioning public sought reassurance that its taxes were being well spent' (Davies et al., 2000: 2) – a concern that clearly remains in these times of budgetary restraints and reduced expenditure on public services.

EBPM became something of a mantra in the United Kingdom with the election of a 'New Labour' government in 1997. In this allegedly post-ideological age, policymaking would be driven by 'what works': what counts is what works. The objectives are radical. The means will be modern. (Labour Party, 1997). The Labour Government's commitment to EBPM was signalled in its 'Modernising Government' White Paper (Cabinet Office, 1999a), which stressed the need for 'better use of evidence in research in policymaking' and the 'Professional Policymaking for the Twenty-first Century' report (Cabinet Office, 1999b), with its four 'big ideas' to help realise the aims of the White Paper – 'peer review', 'joint training events for Ministers and policy makers', 'a policy "knowledge pool"', and 'benchmarks'.

The focus on 'evidence-based' was clear in the establishment of units such as the Centre for Management and Policy Studies (CMPS), the Performance and Innovation Unit and the Social Exclusion Unit. The Cabinet Office explicitly defined evidence as: 'expert knowledge; published research; existing research; stakeholder consultations; previous policy evaluations; the Internet; outcomes from consultations; costings of policy options; output from economic and statistical modelling' (Cabinet Office, 1999a: 33). A series of interventions in welfare delivery, such as the 'New Deals' for the unemployed and 'Sure Start' for preschool children and their families, signalled 'a new approach to the delivery of welfare policies in the United Kingdom and a shift away from the provision of a universal system of welfare to one which is closely targeted on specific groups, and areas' (Wells, 2007: 24, citing Annesley and Gamble, 2004).

The **positivism** inherent in EBPM is contested on two grounds: what is to be counted as 'evidence' and the feasibility of realizing EBPM in a complex world. In terms of 'evidence', there are challenges as to whether it is singular, universal and applicable given the heterogeneity of policy areas. There is fundamental disagreement with the view that certain kinds of 'evidence' should be privileged – those deemed 'scientific' and quantifiable – over other sorts, which are usually more qualitative in nature. Parsons (2002: 3, 8), for example, is critical of the 'knowledge as power model' underpinning EBPM – and EBPM per se – claiming that it 'fails to acknowledge the profound limits of steering in a world in which prediction and control is so difficult and in which "evidence" is so problematic'. There has been criticism, too, that 'evidence' has been discounted by policymakers when it ran counter to their preferred route (Sanderson, 2009: 703).

There is disagreement over whether or not the messy business of politics in a complex world can facilitate a rational arrangement between 'evidence' and policy outputs. The 'ideal' policy process is 'linear, stable and incremental', but this contrasts with the reality of a policymaking environment 'characterized by competition over agenda setting, over jurisdictions, and over interpretations' (Young et al., 2002: 218). Nutley and Webb (2000: 36, 35) identify the 'seven enemies of evidence-based policy' as being 'bureaucratic logic', 'the bottom line', 'consensus', 'politics', 'civil service culture', 'cynicism' and 'time' and call for a more pluralistic, inclusive policy process, wherein many different groups have access to research evidence.

Constructivists challenge EBPM on the grounds that 'knowledge of the social world is socially constructed and culturally and historically contingent' (Sanderson, 2002: 6) and so stress the need for 'experimentation and learning' in policymaking (Sanderson, 2009: 713). 'What works', then, depends on context and interpretation. Post-positivists and institutionalists challenge EBPM's focus on instrumental rationality, arguing instead for the incorporation of ideational phenomena within analyses, especially through policy networks, policy discourses and policy communities.

No one argues that policy should run counter to evidence, but there is disagreement over what 'evidence' means and how it should be used to inform policymaking. It may be that 'evidence-informed policymaking' (EIPM) is a more profitable avenue for exploration than EBPM (Nutley et al., 2007). In such a context, social science research may be used to inform policymaking and not be captured by the agenda of policymakers (Burnham et al., 2008: 325):

> Social Science research should critically examine how societies operate, including the role of government. This involves not only carrying out analyses of how policy and its implementation can be improved, but also looking critically at the actual process of policymaking itself. This may not sit comfortably with the desire of governments to use research to improve their own policy delivery and hence popularity, but it is not a task that can or should be avoided.

evidence-based policy Making (EBPM)

FURTHER READING

Annesley, C. and Gamble, A. (2004) 'Economic and welfare policy', in S. Ludlam and M.J. Smith (eds), *Governing as New Labour: Policy and politics under Blair*. Houndmills, Basingstoke: Palgrave Macmillan.

Burnham, P., Gilland Lutz, K., Grant, W. and Layton-Henry, Z. (2008) *Research Methods in Politics* (2nd edn). Houndmills, Basingstoke: Palgrave Macmillan.

Cabinet Office (1999a) 'Modernising Government'. White Paper Cm 4310. London: The Stationery Office. Also available online at: www.archive.official-documents. co.uk/document/cm43/4310/4310.htm (retrieved 2 April 2012).

Cabinet Office (1999b) 'Professional Policy Making for the Twenty-first Century'. London: Cabinet Office. Also available online via the Digital Education Resource Archive, Institute of Education, University of London at: http://dera.ioe.ac. uk/6320/1/profpolicymaking.pdf (retrieved 2 April 2012).

Campbell Collaboration: www.campbellcollaboration.org

Clarence, E. (2002) 'Technocracy reinvented: The new evidence-based policy movement', *Public Policy and Administration*, 17 (3): 1–11.

Cochrane, A.L. (1972) *Effectiveness and Efficiency: Random reflections on health services*. London: Nuffield Provincial Hospitals Trust.

Davies, H.T.O., Nutley, S.M. and Smith, P.C. (eds) (2000) *What Works?: Evidence-based policy and practice in public services*. Bristol: Policy Press.

Labour Party (1997) 'New Labour because Britain deserves better'. London: Labour Party.

Marston, G. and Watts, R. (2003) 'Tampering with the evidence: A critical appraisal of evidence-based policy making', *An Australian Review of Public Affairs*, 3 (3): 143–63.

Nutley, S.M. and Webb, J. (2000) 'Evidence and the policy process', in H. Davies, S. Nutley and P. Smith (eds), *What Works?: Evidence-based policy and practice in public services*. Bristol: Policy Press. pp. 13–41.

Nutley, S.M., Walter, I. and Davies, H.T.O. (2007) *Using Evidence: How research can inform public services*. Bristol: Policy Press.

Parsons, W. (2002) 'From muddling through to muddling up: Evidence-based policy-making and the modernisation of British government', *Public Policy and Administration*, 17 (3): 43–60.

Sanderson, I. (2002) 'Evaluation, policy learning and evidence-based policy making', *Public Administration*, 80 (1): 1–22.

Sanderson, I. (2009) 'Intelligent policy making for a complex world: Pragmatism, evidence and learning', *Political Studies*, 57 (4): 699–719.

Wells, P. (2007) 'New Labour and evidence-based policy making', *People, Place and Policy Online*, 1 (1): 22–9.

Young, K., Ashby, D., Boaz, A. and Grayson, L. (2002) 'Social science and the evidence-based policy movement', *Social Policy and Society*, 1 (3): 215–24.

EXAMPLES

Biesta, G. (2007) 'Why "what works" won't work: Evidence-based practice and the democratic deficit in educational research', *Educational Theory*, 57 (1): 1–22.

Goldon, B. (2010) 'The sleep of (criminological) reason: Knowledge-policy rupture and New Labour's youth justice legacy', *Criminology and Criminal Justice*, 10 (1): 155–78.

Juntti, M., Russel, D. and Turnpenny, J. (2009) 'Evidence, politics and power in public policy for the environment', *Environmental Science and Policy*, 12 (3): 207–15.

key research concepts in politics & international relations

Feminism/Feminist Methodologies

Feminist research in political science is problem driven rather than method driven and as such is characterised by an eclectic and open-minded approach to methodological questions. (Childs and Krook, 2006: 23)

The purpose of feminist research is to empower women to transform oppressive and exploitative conditions, to provide visions for the future and to attend to the policy complications of research. (Sarantakos, 2004: 68)

What makes feminist researchers feminists? Feminist research is conducted by researchers who are mainly, but not exclusively, women, have a feminist self-identity and feminist perspective. They use multiple research techniques.

Feminist **methodology** attempts to give a voice to women and correct the dominant male-orientated perspective that has developed in social sciences. Many feminist researchers see **positivism** as a male-dominated point of view, with its emphasis on what is perceived to be logical, objective, task-orientated and instrumental. In contrast, feminist research places emphasis on the gradual development of human bonds and accommodation. It sees the political world as a web of interconnected relations with an emphasis on process-orientated goals and inclusivity. Some argue that feminist research has an emancipatory design (see **action research**), meaning that it is not solely focused on recording segments of reality; also, it expresses a personal, political and engaged perspective on the world.

Feminist research argues that the social and political conditions of women's lives are bound in a patriarchal, sexist and 'malestream' society (Stanley and Wise, 1983: 12). The purpose of feminist research, then, is to enlighten others to the gender-blindness around them and practised by them, government and the greater society. It is the *focus* of research that holds together the various fields of feminist research, which is explicitly the commitment to change the position of women in modern societies, study women and employ feminist researchers. As a consequence of feminists viewing the world as dominated by positivism, they employ **qualitative** and/or **quantitative methods**, but it should be

feminism/feminist methodologies

61

stressed that the latter are adjusted to facilitate a focus on the requirements of the feminism **paradigm** – that is, patriarchy, the subjection of
women and power relationships (Sarantakos, 2004: 54).

According to Nielsen (1990), feminist research is 'contextual, inclusive,
experimental, involved, socially relevant, complete but not necessarily
replicable, open to the environment and inclusive of emotions and events
as experienced' (Sarantakos, 2004: 55). Although often these principles
are argued to be **post-positivist**, feminist researchers do not always accept
them. Some will say, for example, that objectivity is missing. Objectivity
is clearly considered to be a part of the requirement for empiricist
research and there are feminist writers who argue that it is possible to be
objective without falling into the positivist framework. It is argued, for
example, that the positivist position of controlling **variables** in research,
detachment and holding a value-neutral position are not acceptable tools
for the feminist whereas other forms of objectivity are. In these cases, the
feminist empiricist research principles are exactly the same as those of
quantitative research: 'she employs a realist ontology; a modified objectivist epistemology; a concern for hypothesis testing, explanation, prediction,
cause–effect linkages, and conventional benchmarks of rigor, including
international and external validity' (Denzin and Lincoln, 1994: 101).
Simply put, the feminist engaged in empirical research will employ the
traditional social science research model, but modify it to avoid the bias
of sexism in order to achieve the feminist standards.

In political research, feminism is extremely diverse – from the empiricist to the postmodern – and the boundaries of feminist research are systematically modelled, defended and utilized by contemporary feminists,
often resting on qualitative research principles. Standpoint feminists
question their research in terms of theories of knowledge. This research
asserts that women, due to their political and personal experiences as
women, are best able to understand the world of women, whether it is the
environment of working life, mothering or the division of labour
(Hartsock, 1998). Although the context of this research changes (race,
class, culture, education or any other factor that causes standpoints to
alter), the common criteria guiding the researcher is the framing of
women within these contexts. Smith (1992: 96) claims that the main
points are standpoint feminist research will:

- provide women with the opportunity to partake in research
- always assert that the researcher is reflexive
- place women's everyday experience at the centre of the research
- build up from women's experiences

- assume a feminist methodology is paramount to understanding women in the world
- reject the traditional research methods as 'malestream'.

With the diverse levels of analysis, research methods and streams of feminist researchers, the question of a distinct feminist methodology has recently been seen as sitting alongside the quantitative, qualitative and critical paradigms. The argument for those in favour of a feminist methodology is that feminism has developed a unique approach, rejecting the *male* paradigm, and it is valid and different from the approaches of other methodologies. Through its rejection of patriarchy, feminist methodology contrasts and can explain political structures, processes and gather results that offer an interpretation only it can provide. For example, Vickers (2006: 85) points to the lack of theory 'needed to bring nations in and to explain nationalism and religion as mobilizers and legitimizers in gendered analyses of political conflict. We even lack a method to map the diversity of women's experiences so we can begin to think systematically about why our experiences differ.'

Elsewhere, researchers have questioned the extent to which a feminist approach to International Relations has 'failed' (Stern and Zalewski, 2009: 625) – specifically in relation to the subfields of security and militarization:

> The widespread acceptance of the need for gendered stories of international political practices might be judged as a measure of feminist success; yet there is an unrelenting set of voices, formally and informally, within the field of International Relations that details and oftentimes bemoans the inability of feminism to deliver the transformative balms it had seemed to promise. Feminist scholarship in International Relations materialises as seemingly stuck in its time of potential, inadequate to theorise successfully, or to 'keep up', and unable to arrive.

Regardless of the power and persuasiveness of these arguments (and many more in support), there is not yet agreement on whether or not the canon can accept the establishment of a feminist methodology. Harding (1987: 188) notes that, given the diversity within feminist research, 'there can never be a feminist science, sociology, anthropology, or epistemology, but only many stories that different women tell about the different knowledge they have'. This methodological eclecticism is celebrated by many as a strength – that is, while there is no feminist methodology per se, there is clearly a distinctive feminist approach to methodology and method (Krook and Squires, 2006: 45).

feminism/feminist methodologies

FURTHER READING

Ackerly, B.A, Stern, M. and True, J. (eds) (2006) *Feminist Methodologies in International Relations*. Cambridge: Cambridge University Press.

Denzin, N.K. and Lincoln, Y.S. (1994) *Handbook of Qualitative Research*. London: Sage.

Harding, S. (1987) *Feminism & Methodology*. Bloomington, IN: Indiana University Press.

Hartsock, N. (1998) *The Feminist Standpoint Revisited and Other Essays*. Oxford: Westview Press.

Reinharz, S. (1992) *Feminist Methods in Social Research*. Oxford: Oxford University Press.

Sarantakos, S. (2004) *Social Research* (3rd edn). Houndmills, Basingstoke: Palgrave Macmillan.

Smith, D. (1992) 'Sociology from women's experience: A reaffirmation', *Sociological Theory*, 10 (1): 88–98.

Stanley, L. and Wise, S. (1983) *Breaking Out: Feminist consciousness and feminist research*. London: Routledge & Kegan Paul.

EXAMPLES

Childs, S.L. and Krook, M.L. (2006) 'Gender and politics: The state of the art', *Politics*, 26 (1): 18–28.

Krook, M.L. and Squires, J.A. (2006) 'Gender quotas in British politics: Multiple approaches and methods in feminist research', *British Politics*, 1 (1): 44–67.

Nielsen, J. (ed.) (1990) *Feminist Research Methods*. Boulder, CO: Westview Press.

Sprague, J. and Hayes, J. (2000) 'Self-determination and empowerment: A feminist standpoint analysis', *American Journal of Community Psychology*, 28 (5): 671–95.

Stern, M. and Zalewski, M. (2009) 'Feminist fatigue(s): Reflections on feminism and familiar fables of militarisation', *Review of International Studies*, 35 (3): 611–30.

Vickers, J. (2006) 'Bringing nations in: Some methodological and conceptual issues in connecting feminisms with nationhood and nationalisms', *International Feminist Journal of Politics*, 8 (1): 84–109.

Focus Groups

For those researchers who are interested in political attitudes, but are uncomfortable with the traditional quantitative or qualitative methodological divide, focus groups present a useful opportunity for gathering data and can be used in combination with other **methods**. Indeed, a mixed methods approach was adopted by White et al. (2001), who used focus groups to supplement nationally representative surveys of Belarusians, Moldovans and Ukrainians in order to understand whether citizens were more likely to favour a West-facing foreign policy (for example, looking towards the European Union and NATO) or an East-facing one (looking towards Russia and the CIS, for instance).

A focus group has several characteristics:

- The number of participants is relatively small – typically between six and ten per group. The number of groups involved will depend on the nature of the study and practical resource issues.
- The researcher leading the group will have a checklist of issues to cover, thereby ensuring that the group does not drift away from the research focus. While asking questions in the same order and using the exact same wording each time is not as important as it is in survey research, Savigny (2007) argues that the behaviour of the group moderator is central to whether we view the data as scientific or not – distinguishing between a positivist 'objective' moderator compared to a more non-directive non-positivist approach.
- The manner in which opinions and attitudes are articulated is of central importance. A focus group is not the same as conducting a number of face-to-face interviews simultaneously. For Fitzpatrick et al. (2000: 498), focus groups supplemented semistructured interviews in 12 case study areas across the UK to develop an appreciation of the nature and effectiveness of youth involvement in urban regeneration. The particular benefit of focus groups in this example were that they 'were found to be a particularly useful form of consultation which, depending on how they were set up, provided the context for personal interaction between decision makers and young people on the latter's "territory"'.
- Focus groups sometimes are used in the planning stage of research. For example, they may help to identify important themes that are then explored in further quantitative and/or qualitative research. This means that **sampling** to ensure representativeness may or may not be crucial to the study.

Focus groups have become an established research technique in the non-political sphere of market research – testing out new products and advertising campaigns – and it comes as no surprise that political parties have adopted similar techniques to test out advertising campaigns

focus groups

and policy proposals. The utilization of focus group research is viewed as one of the successful elements of New Labour's 1997 General Election campaign (Burnham et al., 2004: 105). Bryman (2004) argues that focus groups are particularly useful for researchers using **feminist methodologies**, as:

- more emphasis is placed on group interaction and it is thus less 'artificial' than some other methods relied on by political researchers
- it is less subject to decontextualization than other methods that view research subjects as completely individual entities
- it is less exploitative as it avoids the type of power relationship that can occur in a simple individual researcher–participant scenario – this, too, was an issue for Fitzpatrick's research on young people.

Focus groups offer a viable alternative to survey research in several ways:

- The *quality* of the information is often richer, in that it is possible to understand something about the way in which complex concepts and issues are interpreted. This point was emphasized by Farrell and Gallagher (1999) in their research on voters' attitudes towards electoral systems – a topic that is not the subject of wide debate. Employing focus groups enabled the researchers to first explain the basic principles of different systems, with the discussion demonstrating that views changed as the respondents' information levels rose.
- It may be possible to understand how individuals *rationalize* their opinions and attitudes. For example, 'I don't think I could ever vote for Party X because …'.
- We can appreciate something about the *intensity* of opinion – does a participant stick to an argument or is it subject to the persuasiveness of the arguments of others?
- It tells us something about *group dynamics* and how people respond in the company of others. This is an important aspect of focus group research and it highlights the qualitative aspect of this method – though, of course, in a much more artificial environment than ethnographic methods: 'A key feature of focus groups then is the active encouragement of group interaction among participants. It is the context of the group that is significant' (Savigny, 2007: 126). However, we need to bear in mind that group effects are not a constant feature. For example, it can be difficult to prevent one or two participants from dominating a debate and, equally, particular

research topics may lead to participants 'clamming up' if they believe their opinions will be unpopular.

However, we have to bear in mind that focus groups can be much more time-consuming and costlier to implement than survey research, as well as having other characteristics that need to be taken into account (Burnham et al., 2004: 112):

> The major weakness of focus groups is that it is impossible to know how representative the groups are of the population being researched. No matter how carefully the participants are selected, representativeness cannot be guaranteed. This means that the results are qualitative and indicative rather than valid for the whole population. They will never, therefore, replace surveys and opinion polls as predictors of election results or as sources of data on the state of public opinion.

Researchers are unlikely to rely on the outcomes of a single focus group, however, and careful attention will be given to the composition of different groups. For example, researchers may want to contrast responses in a 'politically active' group with those in a 'politically inactive' group. Marsh et al.'s (2007: 59) work, for instance, utilized focus groups to research a relatively under-researched aspect of political participation research – 'how young people understand and experience politics'. By engaging with 12 focus groups, covering a total of 65 participants, the researchers were able to ensure diversity in relation to sex, ethnicity, socio-economic status, education and contact with the state.

Savigny (2007) challenges the function of focus groups in political research on two counts. First, she asks to what extent do focus groups offer a 'scientific' method for data collection? Here the role of the facilitator is central. While the trained academic researcher may seek to maintain objectivity, this is very different from the stance adopted in political party focus groups, where the facilitator seeks to influence and persuade rather than merely understand.

Savigny's second concern relates to the 'democratizing' nature of focus groups and, again, she draws attention to particular types of focus groups (as utilized by New Labour in its approach to the 1997 General Election) that are not based on representative samples but voters who are likely to switch their voting preference, facilitating what Schattschneider terms the 'mobilisation of bias'.

The fact that the dynamics of the group are of central importance has implications for the recording of data. Focus groups do not require individuals to self-record substantial amounts of information and, in order to fully appreciate the *context* of group dynamics (such as whether someone argues a point very passionately or a participant hesitates to consider his or her wording carefully), Burnham et al. (2004: 110) suggest that video recording focus groups is preferable to making audio recordings. This, though, has resource implications and may influence subsequent behaviour (see **observation** for an explanation of the 'Hawthorne effect').

Focus group research also enables a range of methodological innovations that are less common (though not excluded) from survey and interview research. Referring again to Marsh et al.'s (2007: 76) research, their focus groups facilitated what they refer to as the *vignette* method, in which participants were shown a range of images to provoke discussion around political themes: 'The strength of the method as far as our research was concerned was that it allowed respondents to interpret the image and the subject matter of the interview, in this case politics, according to their own experiences and priorities ... In addition, some of our respondents had lower levels of literacy and texts were not a commonly used medium to them', thus indicating that written instructions or information to facilitate debate is not always feasible in research.

It appears, then, that there are particular areas of political research which benefit from a focus group **methodology**. This may be when:

- there is a worry about the possibility of exploitation of power relationships (for example, of women or young people)
- there is a need to try alternative methods of engagement – engaging local communities in decision-making has, more recently, placed greater emphasis on focus groups, citizens' panels, community visioning exercises and deliberative polling alongside the more traditional approach of inviting local lay people onto partnership boards or committees (Sykes and Hedges, 1998, cited in Fitzpatrick et al., 2000)
- the subject matter is one that needs some explanation and contextualization.

It is important, however, that we recognize the differences in the processes used for focus groups conducted for ostensibly academic research and the processes used for those which are underpinned by a far more 'political' motivation.

FURTHER READING

Bryman, A. (2004) *Social Research Methods* (2nd edn). Oxford: Oxford University Press. Chapter 16.

Burnham, P., Gilland Lutz, K., Grant, W. and Layton-Henry, Z. (2004) *Research Methods in Politics*. Houndmills, Basingstoke: Palgrave Macmillan. pp. 105–12.

Stewart, D.W., Shamdasani, P.N. and Rook, D.W. (2007) *Focus Groups: Theory and practice* (2nd edn). London: Sage.

EXAMPLES

Farrell, D.M. and Gallagher, M. (1999) 'British voters and their criteria for evaluating electoral systems', *The British Journal of Politics and International Relations*, 1 (3): 293–316.

Fitzpatrick, S., Hastings, A. and Kintrea, K. (2000) 'Youth involvement in urban regeneration: Hard lessons, future directions', *Policy & Politics*, 28 (4): 493–509.

Marsh, D., O'Toole, T. and Jones, S. (2007) *Young People and Politics in the UK: Apathy or alienation?* Houndmills, Basingstoke: Palgrave Macmillan.

Savigny, H. (2007) 'Focus groups and political marketing: Science and democracy as axiomatic?', *The British Journal of Politics and International Relations*, 9 (1): 122–37.

Schattschneider, E. E. (1960) *The Semi-sovereign People*. New York: Holt, Reinhart and Winston.

White, S., Light, M. and Lowenhardt, J. (2001) 'Belarus, Moldova and Ukraine: Looking east or looking west?', *Perspectives on European Politics and Society*, 2 (2): 289–304.

Hypothesis Testing and Inference

As Politics and International Relations belong to the generic group of social sciences we are unable to establish hard and fast rules about the behaviour of **variables** in the way that we can in the world of the natural sciences. The 'laws' of political behaviour or political organizations are not laws in the sense that they are understood in physics – there is far less opportunity for certainty and predictability.

A common feature of debates around the value of **quantitative** and **qualitative methods** surrounds the issue of generalizability – the extent to which the results of one investigation can be applied to similar political cases, countries, cultures or societies. The research process frequently requires us to make inferences (see **sampling**) – as research populations may be too large or subject to limited accessibility – and, as such, we can study a section of, rather than a whole, phenomenon. Within quantitative political research, inferences are strongly associated with hypothesis testing, in which we use samples and statistical tests based on levels of significance to establish the relationship between **concepts**. Sampling (and certainly random sampling) does not have the same priority for those engaged in qualitative research and, as a result, incorrect inferences that emanate from non-random samples are more likely to appear.

Elsewhere in this text (see **empirical analysis** and **epistemology**) we have drawn your attention to research approaches that favour either a deductive or inductive approach. Hypothesis testing is closely related to the deductive method – that is, we have a 'suspicion' deriving from existing theory or evidence which we seek to test: 'The proposition, or research hypothesis, usually relates two concepts and is specified in a way such that it could either be true or false … The characteristics of a working hypothesis are that it is precise, testable against data and potentially falsifiable' (Fielding and Gilbert, 2000: 243).

Payne and Payne (2004: 113–14) identify four characteristics common to hypotheses in social research. A hypothesis:

- is a statement, not a question (for example, 'Those over 50 are more likely to vote than those under 30 years of age', rather than 'Does age affect electoral turnout?')
- should refer to a single relation between concepts, hence studies often test multiple hypotheses – one at a time
- should be clearly stated and logically consistent
- should be empirically testable.

It will come as little surprise that hypothesis testing is a feature of quantitative research. Fielding and Gilbert identify four stages to hypothesis testing:

- Making appropriate assumptions – it is important to bear in mind that we can never be absolutely sure we have made the right decision in accepting or rejecting our hypothesis. As Popper argued, we can never prove something in social research with absolute confidence, though we can be confident in rejecting a claim as being untrue. If we are unable to support the working hypothesis, then we accept the *null hypothesis* and claim that no relationship between the variables exists. When establishing our hypothesis, we need to decide whether to carry out a one-tailed or two-tailed test.

- Selecting a test statistic – whether we use a one-tailed or two-tailed test will depend on what we intend to examine. If, for example, we establish a working hypothesis that states those aged 50 and above are more likely to vote than those under the age of 30, then this would be a one-tailed test. However, if we were to claim that we expect a difference between turnout for the two age groups – but not necessarily what that difference will be – this would be a two-tailed test. If we reject the null hypothesis when, in fact, there is not a relationship between the two variables, then this is referred to as a *type I error* – that is, rejecting a null hypothesis that is true. However, if we accept the null hypothesis when, in fact, there is a relationship between two variables, we have made a *type II error* – that is, rejecting a working hypothesis that is true. In political research this can often occur when we have failed to choose appropriate samples. In deciding whether to accept or reject the hypothesis we generally refer to our confidence at the *5 per cent significance level*. This means that there is a 1 in 20 chance we will inappropriately accept the working hypothesis (as the sample is not representative of the research population). If we want to increase our confidence in rejecting the null hypothesis, we can use the *1 per cent significance level* – though this increases the chances that we make a type II error.
- Compute the test statistic – the test we use depends on certain data qualities. It is unnecessary to go into detail here, but there are many statistical texts that will enable you to identify the correct test to use.
- Accepting or rejecting the hypothesis – bearing in mind what we have said about confidence levels, we can never be absolutely sure we have made the correct decision.

Turning to the principle underpinning inference, Burnham et al. (2004: 144) state that it is the same for quantitative and qualitative research, 'but the application of that principle differs greatly between them'. Referring to the work of King et al. (1994), they distinguish between:

- descriptive inferences – the use of available data to create a systematic description, which is the dominant type of inference in political research

- causal inferences – this relates to the generation of 'laws', in the sense that one event or feature will lead to another, so, for example, we might infer that a prolonged period of unfavourable poll ratings will lead to pressure on a political leader to resign.

The term 'hypothesis' is used much less frequently in qualitative analysis, though we should not, as a result, mistakenly believe that it is entirely absent. Rather, a hypothesis is more likely to emerge through an inductive approach – data is studied, hypotheses are developed and these hypotheses are refined through further data analysis.

FURTHER READING

Burnham, P., Gilland Lutz, K., Grant, W. and Layton-Henry, Z. (2004) *Research Methods in Politics*. Houndmills, Basingstoke: Palgrave Macmillan. Chapter 6.
Fielding, J. and Gilbert, N. (2000) *Understanding Social Statistics*. London: Sage.
King, G., Keohane, R. O. and Verba, S. (1994) *Designing Social Enquiry*. Princeton, NJ: Princeton University Press.
Payne, G. and Payne, J. (2004) *Key Concepts in Research Methods*. London: Sage.

EXAMPLES

Foweraker, J. and Landman, T. (2004) 'Economic development and democracy revisited: Why dependency theory is not yet dead', *Democratization*, 11 (1): 1–20.
Hammond, T.H. and Butler, C.K. (2003) 'Some complex answers to the simple question "Do institutions matter?": Policy choice and policy change in presidential and parliamentary systems', *Journal of Theoretical Politics*, 15 (2):145–200.
Popper, K. (1963) *Conjectures and Refutations: The Growth of Scientific Knowledge*, London: Routledge

key research concepts in
politics & international relations

.... Interviewing ....

Interviews provide an excellent opportunity to explore a political actor's beliefs, motivations and processes of decision-making. In addition to asking 'What?'-style questions we can probe responses with 'Why?' and similar contextual cues. For interpretivists such as Seale (1998: 204–5), interviews are an obvious preferred method – avoiding the potentially exploitative scenario created by standardized **survey designs** in which 'an unequal, unbalanced relationship was thereby set up, where the researcher possessed all the power to define what was relevant and what was irrelevant'. In addition, Stedward (1997: 151) claims:

> In particular, the interview is a great vehicle for bringing a research topic to life. It is also an excellent method of obtaining data about contemporary subjects which have not been extensively studied and for which there is little literature.

Seldon (1988: 4) noted, 'Interviews can be particularly helpful in fleshing out documents when it comes to reconstructing the roles and methods of personalities, and their relationships with others.'

Interviews follow a schedule, becoming more qualitative in nature as they become less 'formalized'. For example, a 'standardized' interview schedule typically takes the form of a questionnaire – participants are asked precisely the same questions in the same order and generate short answers that are suitable for coding for quantitative analytical purposes. These are the least conversational in nature. In a structured interview, the goal is to obtain answers to clearly defined questions, which allows for uniformity and the results are then readily comparable. A 'semi-standardized' interview schedule is frequently used to prompt **focus group** discussions – the format being more flexible in recognition of the fact that some issues may deserve more exploration. 'Unstandardized' interviews are characteristically unstructured, making them useful for collecting oral histories and in-depth detail. They should be highly conversational and involve relatively little intervention from the interviewer (though we should not make the mistake of confusing unstructured with unprepared – these are very different). In-depth interviews also encourage the capturing of the participants' perceptions and wording, both of which can be invaluable to qualitative data collection as they allow researchers to present the meaningfulness of the experience from the participants' position.

High-quality interviews require a good deal of experience and skill on the part of the interviewer. There is a danger that the conversation can drift towards rambling waffle if there are not a few well-placed interjections to help focus the mind (think here of the skills of veteran professional presenters who constantly press politicians to answer the question asked rather than one they would prefer to answer). A good interviewer will follow an aide mémoire, which is a series of thematic prompts but these lack the rigid structure of a closed questionnaire. A successful

interviewing

interview should allow the interviewer to 'get under the skin' of the interviewee – we look for motivations, rationales and justifications.

Interviewing involves some practical obstacles. First, there is the question of access – how do we convince someone to give up a decent portion of their time to answer our enquiries? We are often driven to carry out interviews with people because we deem them to be 'important' – they have first-hand experience of an event, organisation, process – or they may be decision-makers themselves – we are interested in their views because they are important to others. With this in mind, we might encounter 'gatekeepers' – those assistants and administrators who keep diaries and manage day-to-day access to elites. For inexperienced interviewers, initial encounters can be daunting and a test of skill – it is important that we do not interview key participants too early and risk failing to collect the information that we most need.

A second issue is location. Where people complete a questionnaire may not be a key concern. In fact, we probably want them to take their time to answer fully, so would prefer it if they completed one at their convenience. In contrast, an interview generally involves researchers 'going' to their interviewees for a prearranged meeting. If we are fortunate, we may have a quiet room and time to discuss, but it may also be the case that we are interviewing while on the move, in the time between commitments in their busy schedules. This has substantial implications for how many interviews we can expect to complete in a modest timeframe. This said, feminists have drawn attention to the positive need to consider location. Oakley (1982), for example, claims that interviewing women in an environment with which they are comfortable is less exploitative than some more formal approaches to research.

A third concern (and not unrelated to location) is how an interview is recorded. Ideally, we would wish to capture an interview by audio/video recording, but often this is impractical or undesirable. In the classic political study *Political Ideology*, Lane (1962: 9) made audio recordings of his series of interviews with the typical American urban man as, 'by the use of a tape recorder the interviews provided a *textual* account of everything said. The choice of words employed, the hesitations between words, the style and language of discourse were all revealed in the transcript'. In contrast, others see recording as a 'controversial tool' (Manheim and Rich, 1995: 167). Interviewees might find recording equipment intrusive and offputting and, if the interview is being conducted 'on the go' and in a public space, the quality of the recording may be compromised. Recorded interviews also need to be transcribed. Without the services of a professional transcriber this can be a resource-intensive process for researchers to undertake themselves (it takes at least five hours to transcribe a 60-minute interview), though the advantage is that, once transcribed, such material can be analysed by qualitative software programs, such as NVivo.

In conclusion, there are three requirements that need to be met in order for interviews to be successful:

- accessibility – the value of good contacts and pushing past gatekeepers should not be underestimated
- objectivity – to ensure that the information gathered is fit for the purposes of the research
- resources – in the form of time and possibly the finances required to travel and so on.

From the outset, we will probably have to acknowledge that our information is not representative of broader sociopolitical groups and it may be (intentionally or unintentionally) biased and subject to human error (particularly if we are asking interviewees to recall reasonably historical events).

FURTHER READING

Aberbach, J. and Rockman, B. (2002) 'Conducting and coding elite interviews', *PS: Political Science and Politics*, 24: 673–6.

Berry, J. (2002) 'Validity and reliability in elite interviewing', *PS: Political Science and Politics*, 24: 679–82.

Burnham, P., Gilland Lutz, K., Grant, W. and Layton-Henry, Z. (2008) *Research Methods in Politics* (2nd edn). Houndmills, Basingstoke: Palgrave Macmillan. Chapter 9.

Goldstein, K. (2002) 'Getting in the door: Sampling and completing elite interviews', *PS: Political Science and Politics*, 24: 669–72.

Harrison, L. (2001) *Political Research: An introduction*. Abingdon: Routledge. Chapter 6.

Keats, D. (2000) *Interviewing: A practical guide for students and professionals*. Buckingham: Open University Press.

Lilleker, D. (2003) 'Interviewing the political elite: Navigating the political minefield', *Politics*, 23 (3): 207–14.

Manheim, J. and Rich, R.C. (1995) *Empirical Political Analysis* (4th edn). New York: Longman. Chapter 8.

McCracken, G. (1988) *The Long Interview*. London: Sage.

Richards, D. (1996) 'Elite interviewing: Approaches and pitfalls', *Politics*, 16 (3): 199–204.

Seale, C. (ed.) (1998) *Researching Society and Culture*. London: Sage.

Seldon, A. (1998) *Contemporary History: Practice and method*. Oxford: Blackwell.

Stedward, G. (1997) 'On the record: An introduction to interviewing', in P. Burnham (ed.), *Surviving the Research Process in Politics*. London: Pinter.

interviewing

EXAMPLES

Bale, T. (1996) 'Interview material in political science', *Politics*, 16 (1): 63–7.

Childs, S. (2001) 'In their own words: New Labour women and the substantive representation of women', *The British Journal of Politics and International Relations*, 3 (2): 173–90.

Childs, S. (2002) 'Hitting the target: Are Labour women MPs "acting for" women?', *Parliamentary Affairs*, 55 (1): 143–53.

Crewe, I. and King, A. (1995) *SDP: The birth, life and death of the Social Democratic Party*. Oxford: Oxford University Press.

Davies, P. (2001) 'Spies as informants: Triangulation and the interpretation of elite interview data in the study of the intelligence and security services', *Politics*, 21 (1): 73–80.

Farrell, D. and Gallagher, M. (1999) 'British voters and their criteria for evaluating electoral systems', *British Journal of Politics and International Relations*, 1 (3): 293–316.

Heclo, H. and A. Wildavsky (1981) *The Private Government of Public* Money (2nd edn). London: Macmillan.

Lane, R. (1962) *Political Ideology: Why the American common man believes what he does*. New York: Free Press of Glencoe.

Levy, M. (1996) 'Modernization and the Clause IV Reform: The attitudes of Labour backbench MPs', in D.M. Farrell, D. Broughton, D. Denver and J. Fisher (eds), *The British Elections and Parties Yearbook 1996*. London: Frank Cass.

McEvoy, J. (2006) 'Elite interviewing in a divided society: Lessons from Northern Ireland', *Politics*, 26 (3): 184–91.

Oakley, A. (1982) 'Interviewing women: A contradiction in terms', in H. Roberts (ed.), *Doing Feminist Research*. London: Routledge.

Ross, K. (2001) 'Political elites and the pragmatic paradigm: Notes from a feminist researcher – in the field and out to lunch', *International Journal of Social Research Methodology*, 4 (2): 155–66.

Ward, R. (2002) 'Invisible women: The political roles of unionist and loyalist women in contemporary Northern Ireland', *Parliamentary Affairs*, 55 (1): 167–78.

.... Levels of Measurement ......

When engaging in **quantitative analysis** we make use of numerical data. However, the information, or **variables**, in which we are interested are not always quantitative in their original format. Think, for example, of someone's political party preference – this is the name of a party rather than a number. However, some variables are quantitative – for example, someone's age. Also, for analytical purposes, we frequently code responses in order to assist with description and **correlation**. Indeed, if you are familiar with statistical analysis packages such as SPSS, you already will be aware that variables have to be given numerical codes. When applying numerical values to political variables, we can utilize a range of measurement levels. It is possible to recategorize the more detailed levels (such as interval and ratio) of data into lower levels, but we cannot do the reverse (that is, if the data is ordinal, we cannot make it richer). Therefore, particularly in relation to primary analysis, it is important to give some consideration to what type of data would be most useful and informative for a research project before establishing which data-collection mechanisms to use.

The four levels of measurement are:

- categorical/nominal
- ordinal
- interval
- ratio.

Categorical/nominal is the most basic level. As the label suggests, it involves placing data into discrete, mutually exclusive categories. There is no relative value to the categories – that is, we cannot say they are stronger or better than others. Some examples of such data are a respondent's sex and which candidate was voted for in a simple plurality election. In addition, it is common when presenting data on variables such as age and income for researchers to employ categories. This is because we are usually interested in what we might call 'cohort' or 'generational' trends (do those labelled 'baby boomers' differ in their politics from those called 'Thatcher's children') rather than whether those who are 35 years of age are very different from those who are 37.

An example of this approach can be seen in the work of Pattie et al. (2003) in their analysis of the Citizen Audit. In presenting trend data, they employ four age categories (25 and under, 26–45, 46–65, 66 and over) and eight household income categories (under £10,000, £10,000–£19,999, £20,000–£29,999 and so on). Although we put numerical labels on categories, we should bear in mind that those labels have no arithmetic value. As a result, a 'frequency count is the only quantitative operation that is meaningful with categorical data' (Burnham et al., 2004: 117).

Ordinal is the level at which we find data that is ranked. For example, we may present respondents with a list of political issues (such as economic stability, reducing hospital waiting lists, tougher criminal sentences, reducing carbon footprints) and ask that they rate them in order of preference. Similarly, we can place election candidates in order of preference. However, we have to bear in mind that the 'distance' between places or preferences may not be equal for each instance. I may rank tougher criminal sentences as my first priority and economic stability as my second, but that does not necessarily mean crime is twice as important to me as the state of the economy. Ordinal scales are frequently used in political research to test the intensity of opinion regarding a policy, organization or personality. The British Election Study (BES) 2005 Campaign questionnaire, for example, included the following question and closed options:

How well do you think the present government has handled crime in Britain?

Very well

Fairly well

Neither well nor badly

Fairly badly

Very badly

Don't know

While people's responses help us to appreciate the strength of opinion on the topic, we cannot claim that 'very well' is twice the strength of 'fairly well' – we cannot confidently claim these are equidistant. A further example is provided by Bechhofer and McCrone (2007) who examine social attitudes towards national identity by asking questions that require respondents to identify themselves as British, Scottish, English and so on. This research utilizes the 'Moreno question' in which respondents select one identity from a hierarchical range – such as 'Scottish, not British', 'More Scottish than British' and 'Equally Scottish and British'. The 'more' has no numerical value.

Interval data (alongside ratio levels) are those we see as being most informative as we can appreciate something about the distances between variables. Interval data does not have a meaningful zero point. Grades for an assessment are an example of interval data. So, we can say that someone with a mark of 60 has performed substantially better than someone with a mark of 30, but it does not necessarily mean the paper was twice as good. Note, though, that we could transform assessment grades for a class into ordinal scores (ranking by performance) or nominal scores (grouped by firsts, upper seconds, lower seconds and so on).

The main distinction between ratio and interval data is that ratio data has a meaningful zero point. Age is an example of ratio data – we cannot have a minus age. Someone who is 40 is twice as old as someone who is 20. In political research, ratio levels of measurement are more common than interval levels of measurement.

In order to appreciate how 'typical' any case is in relation to a variable, in general, we employ measures of central tendency (Burnham et al., 2004: 119). If we ask a question such as 'What is the average age of voters?' or 'Typically, how do respondents rate the government's handling of crime?', then we can employ three different measures:

- mean – the arithmetic average, which can be applied to interval- and ratio-level data
- median – the middle value when scores are placed in ascending to descending order, which can be applied to ordinal-, interval- and ratio-level data
- mode – the most frequently occurring value, which can be applied to categorical-/nominal-, ordinal-, interval- and ratio-level data.

When examining the relationships between different levels of measurement, we can use a number of statistical tests. Our choice of test will be influenced by the nominal, ordinal and interval/ratio categories. The tests, and when we should employ them, are outlined below.

Table 1 Examples of statistical tests

Test	Conditions
Chi-squared	At least one variable is nominal
Spearman's rho	Both variables are ordinal or one is ordinal and one is interval/ratio
Pearson's r	Both variables are interval/ratio

FURTHER READING

Burnham, P., Gilland Lutz, K., Grant, W. and Layton-Henry, Z. (2004) *Research Methods in Politics*. Houndmills, Basingstoke: Palgrave Macmillan. pp. 116–19.

Harrison, L. (2001) *Political Research: An introduction*. Abingdon: Routledge. pp. 17–19.

EXAMPLES

Bechhofer, F. and McCrone, D. (2007) 'Being British: A crisis of identity?', *The Political Quarterly*, 78 (2): 251–60.

John, P. and Margetts, M. (2009) 'The latent support for the extreme Right in British politics', *West European Politics*, 32 (3): 496–513.

Pattie, C., Seyd, P. and Whiteley, P. (2003) 'Civic attitudes and engagement in modern Britain', *Parliamentary Affairs*, 56 (4): 616–33.

Plug, W., Zeijl, E. and Du Bois-Reymond, M. (2003) 'Young people's perceptions of youth and adulthood: A longitudinal study from The Netherlands', *Journal of Youth Studies*, 6 (2): 127–44.

Pollock, G., Antcliff, V. and Ralphs, R. (2002) 'Work orders: Analysing employment histories using sequence data', *International Journal of Social Research Methodology*, 5 (2): 91–105.

Methods

When referring to a research method, or methods, we are concerned with the tools that inform the data-collection and analysis processes. As Landman (2000: 15) states, method 'is the means by which a theory is derived and tested, including the collection of evidence, formulation and testing of hypotheses, and the arrival at substantive conclusions'. It involves collecting data to address research questions.

What we want to know will be influenced by our position on what there is to know (our ontological stance) and how we may best know it (our epistemological stance). Researchers with a positivist position will tend towards using more **quantitative methods** and a

deductive approach. Researchers within the interpretivist tradition are more inclined to use **qualitative methods** and an **inductive** research approach.

While it is common to distinguish between what are classified as predominantly quantitative methods and qualitative methods, this may incorrectly give the impression that one approach is superior to the other or they are mutually exclusive research tools (see **triangulation**). The methods are not irreconcilable and a mixed methods approach can facilitate a more thorough understanding of phenomena than is possible using one method alone. Hester et al. (2010: 251) also note:

> Methods are situated historically. They not only reflect the socio-economic context and concerns of different eras, but have developed and changed over time as different interest groups and needs have emerged ... Different research traditions have consequently developed in different parts of the world and at different times, and different methods have also achieved differential degrees of credibility and impact.

While particular methods may be utilized to a greater or lesser extent in political and international relations research, many of the 'rules' of operationalizing methods apply across the social sciences – that is, the rules applying to **survey design** apply whether we are sociologists or political scientists. Rather than choosing a method and then developing a research question, it is more appropriate to focus first on what we want to know, then select a method that is best suited to acquiring the 'right sort of data', as (Hay, 2002: 252):

> the object of the natural scientist's analytical attentions remains independent of the analytical process in a way which is simply not the case for the analysis of social and political systems. The latter are populated by conscious and reflective agents who are capable of revising their behaviour, often in the light of – and even in direct response to – the theories advanced by social and political analysts. There is no equivalent in the natural sciences.

Choice of research method is influenced by several factors. First, the method will be informed and directed by the research question. Are we asking questions that reflect a 'what', 'why' or 'how'? 'What?' can often

methods

be answered by relatively simplistic descriptive quantitative data (such as turnout figures at elections to act as an indicator as to political participation) or by qualitative observation (noting who tends to lead discussions in meetings, for example).

A move towards more complex questions addressing 'Why?' and 'How?' requires more advanced methods. We might, for example, use multiple regression analysis of large-scale quantitative data sets, qualitative interviews and ethnographic studies. In the field of foreign policy analysis, for example, researchers often have been interested in why policymakers made a specific decision at a particular time. The research question, then, may involve looking at both the external context of the decision but also at internal factors that may have influenced the decisionmakers' agency, such as their cognitions: 'the beliefs and reasoning processes of individuals [which] matter because they underlie all political behavior and form the foundation for how both power and interests are understood' (Young and Schafer, 1998: 64). It is challenging, however, to evaluate the impact of cognitions and, consequently, a variety of research methods have been deployed, such as **content analysis**, **discourse analysis** and **interviewing** (Dyson, 2006; Hermann, 1980).

Second, which method is chosen will be determined by the resources available for data collection, particularly whether the intention is to analyse primary or secondary data. In the case of the latter, we might find that the questions we can ask are, to some extent, defined by what exists. A strength of engaging with secondary data is that the method is non-reactive – we are unable to affect the behaviour and thoughts of those being studied as we are not in direct contact with them as researchers.

Third, we can distinguish between methods we use when studying single cases as opposed to when we are using **comparative methods**. In relation to the latter, Landman (2000: 22) identifies a trade-off between level of abstraction and scope of countries. The greater the range of countries chosen to include in a study of a particular political **concept**, the less specific we can be in its conceptualization. For example, if we decided to compare the different types of electoral systems in a region rather than between two countries only – we would need to have a wider range of categories of electoral systems to capture the distinctive features of each of the systems and so our working definition of 'electoral system' would be more stretched and less precise.

Fourth, when choosing methods, we should take note of debates about their relative strengths and weaknesses, as well as approaches adopted by similar existing studies – replicating a study with similar methods is one way to establish the **reliability** of your findings.

The 'appropriateness' of specific methods may not be a static concept. Ethical considerations may result in certain methods going out of favour, while technological developments may enable researchers to utilize innovative and more effective methods. Research involving people has become the focus of increased consideration of **ethics** and political scientists have historically not been subject to the same strict regulations that have been applied to psychologists and, more recently, sociologists. In particular, we need to pay attention to the duties of researchers to maintain participants' confidentiality and the importance of informed consent. Gone are the days of Milgram's psychological experiments, in which participants thought they were dispensing life-threatening electric shocks to fellow humans. The challenge of methodological appropriateness can be seen in the development of a view of research as performative practice, where performativity is 'the reiterative and citational practice through which discourse produces the effects that it names' (Butler 1993: 2). As a result, 'If we think of research (or the creation of new discourse) in this light, emphasis shifts away from notions like objectivity and truth to an interrogation of the potential effects of research' (Gibson et al., 2001: 366).

In relation to methodological innovations, we have witnessed a growing trust in the value of Internet surveys. A common concern for those conducting surveys has been the decline in response rates, but Orr cites examples of Internet **survey designs** that have benefited from better response rates than the more traditional mail surveys. Orr (2005: 263) states that, 'While web surveys require respondents to have Internet access, which precludes conducting general population surveys via the web, in fact many of the populations of interest to political scientists such as interest groups, elected officials, and bureaucrats have near universal access to the web.' Indeed, Internet surveys formed a significant element of the 2005 and 2010 British Election Studies (alongside established face-to-face methods).

Fielding (2010) argues that the preference for mixed methods research (MMR) in government-commissioned research has had implications for qualitative methods. Fielding alludes to large-scale and high-profile applied research (such as the American government's class action tobacco lawsuits) having facilitated the development of (qualitative) data management software. In turn, this has led to the formalization of explicit research quality standards. For example, in the UK, the Government Social Research (GSR) competency framework was first published in 2005 to signal the expectations regarding standards for government researchers. However, a challenge for Fielding is this normalization of a 'checklist' approach. As he (2010: 133) argues, the standards established for quantitative research have been both established for longer and were derived from a more obvious consensus: 'explicit quality criteria emerged from the technical apparatus of quantitative work and were learned in training'.

FURTHER READING

Fielding, N. (2010) 'Mixed methods research in the real world', *International Journal of Social Research Methodology*, 13 (2): 127–38.

Hay, C. (2002) *Political Analysis: A critical introduction*. Houndmills, Basingstoke: Palgrave Macmillan.

Landman, T. (2000) *Issues and Methods in Comparative Politics: An introduction*. Abingdon: Routledge.

EXAMPLES

Butler, J. (1993) *Bodies that Matter: On the discursive limits of 'sex'*. Abingdon: Routledge.

Dyson, S.B. (2006) 'Personality and foreign policy: Tony Blair's Iraq decisions', *Foreign Policy Analysis*, 2 (3): 289–306.

Gibson, K., Law, L. and McKay, D. (2001) 'Beyond heroes and victims: Filipina contract migrants, economic activism and class transformations', *International Feminist Journal of Politics*, 3 (3): 365–86.

Hermann, M.G. (1980) 'Explaining foreign policy behavior using the personal characteristics of political leaders', *International Studies Quarterly*, 24 (1): 7–46.

Hester, M., Donovan, C. and Fahmy, E. (2010) 'Feminist epistemology and the politics of method: Surveying same sex domestic violence', *International Journal of Social Research Methodology*, 13 (3): 251–63.

Orr, S.K. (2005) 'New technology and research: An analysis of internet survey methodology in political science', *PS: Political Science and Politics*, 38 (2): 263–7.

Young, M.D. and Schafer, M. (1998) 'Is there method in our madness?: Ways of assessing cognition in international relations', *Mershon International Studies Review*, 42 (1): 63–96.

Methodology

> Small differences in methodology can yield big differences in results …
> Methodology is about knowing and showing that we are right when we
> make claims. It owes as much to the world of legal reasoning as it does to
> the world of natural science. (Aspinwall, 2006: 5–6)

While **method** refers to the specific tools of research (such as **surveys**, **interviewing** and **documentary analysis**), methodology is a much broader term, relating to epistemological concerns and philosophical assumptions. According to Grix (2002: 179), methodology logically precedes research methods. Hay (2002: 63) summarizes the link between **ontology**, **epistemology** and methodology precisely by stating that 'their relationship is directional in the sense that ontology logically precedes epistemology which logically precedes methodology'. Moses and Knutsen (2007: 5) refer to these as the 'three musketeers of metaphysics', in which methodology 'denotes an investigation of the concepts, theories and basic principles of reasoning on the subject'.

It is not unusual, then, to see certain methodological traditions within competing fields of research, but it is important that we do not take the usefulness or appropriateness of methodology as given. Students of International Relations will be familiar with approaches favouring **realism**, liberalism/pluralism and globalization/Marxism, while in Political Science we are just as likely to refer to approaches such as institutionalism, **behaviouralism** and **feminism**. There is much to be said for methodological pluralism, which 'treats all methods as equal, assessing the merits of any given method in terms of how appropriately it tackles the research task on hand' (Payne and Payne, 2004: 149), but, as can be seen in the entries on **behaviouralism** and **feminism**, there is a tendency for different approaches to prefer particular methods. This gives rise to debates on methodology within the subject area.

One such prominent debate within International Relations was between feminist researchers and positivists. Keohane (1998: 197) called for feminists in the field to adopt a research programme 'specifying their propositions, and providing systematically gathered evidence to test these propositions', advising that the 'scientific method, in the broadest sense, is the best path towards convincing current nonbelievers of the validity of the message that feminists are seeking to deliver'.

This identification of feminist research as inherently wedded to non-quantitative research methods is rejected by Caprioli (2004: 255, 253) who claims that 'space exists within the field for feminist enquiry' and that 'Quantitative methodology and feminism are not mutually exclusive'. Finch (2004: 61), too, points out that 'there is, despite what many have argued, no essential link between feminism and qualitative research, and probably there have been some significant disadvantages to both feminist insights and qualitative research, from this link having developed in such a close fashion.' Hughes and Cohen (2010: 190) echo such sentiments, stating, 'it is crucial that we escape these simplistic dichotomies and re-open quantitative methodologies to critical feminist epistemology and feminist empirics'.

Just as specific methods may shift in and out of favour, so, too, may methodologies. For example, Haubrich (2006) contends that the methodology of analysing the political has been affected by the new threat of transnational terrorism (post-September 11 2001). In particular, his concern focuses on the fact that 'There is a widespread consensus in the academy, however, that what occurs at home is distinct from that abroad, and that both should be examined separately from each other, so that the "outside" of a society is left to the discipline of international relations, while the "inside" with its more formal domestic responsibilities is assigned to political studies broadly conceived' (2006: 84). The traditionally clear division between the domestic and the international is no longer distinct.

In their study of comparative politics, van Biezen and Caramani (2006) argue that comparative politics in Britain is dominated by single-country studies, while the methodology-orientated and the analytical comparative traditions are more strongly developed in the United States and continental Europe respectively. What, though, does a 'methodology-orientated' tradition mean? van Biezen and Caramani (2006: 31) answer this question as follows:

> At the heart of the methodology-oriented tradition is a concern with the potential of comparative politics to provide causal explanations of political phenomena … Part of the methodology-oriented tradition is concerned with the issue of concept formation, a field of inquiry in the social sciences closely associated with the work of Giovanni Sartori … A

second strand deals with methodological issues such as the reliability of measurements and indicators, the rules for case selection, the development of probabilistic explanatory models and so on ... While impressive for its methodological and statistical sophistication, however, work in this tradition may run the risk of elevating technique over substance.

Researchers, then, are likely to discuss the 'rights and wrongs' of methods in relation to specific research questions, but are more relaxed about accepting the trend for 'methodological turns'. Essentially, methodological pluralism is accepted as a fundamental feature of social science research. For example, Little (1991) draws attention to the methodological debate within International Relations sparked by Waltz's *Theory of International Politics* when it was published in 1979.

FURTHER READING

Aspinwall, M. (2006) 'Studying the British', *Politics*, 26 (1): 3–10.

Grix, J. (2002) 'Introducing students to the generic terminology of social research', *Politics*, 22 (3): 175–86.

Payne, G. and Payne, J. (2004) *Key Concepts in Research Methods*. London: Sage.

EXAMPLES

Caprioli, M. (2004) 'Feminist IR theory and quantitative methodology: A critical analysis', *International Studies Review*, 6 (2): 253–69.

Finch, J. (2004) 'Feminism and qualitative research', *International Journal of Social Research Methodology*, 7 (1): 61–4.

Haubrich, D. (2006) 'The foreign v. the domestic after September 11th: The methodology of political analysis revisited', *Politics*, 26 (2): 84–92.

Hay, C. (2002) *Political Analysis: A critical introduction*. Houndmills, Basingstoke: Palgrave Macmillan.

Hughes, C. and Cohen, L. (2010) 'Feminists really do count: The complexity of feminist methodologies', *International Journal of Social Research Methodology*, 13 (3): 189–96.

Keohane, R.O (1998) 'Beyond dichotomy: Conversations between international relations and feminist theory', *International Studies Quarterly*, 42 (1): 193–7.

Kornprobst, M. (2009) 'International relations as rhetorical discipline: Toward (re) newing horizons', *International Studies Review*, 11 (1): 87–108.

Little, R. (1991) 'International relations and the methodological turn', *Political Studies*, 39 (3): 463–78.

Moses, J.W. and Knutsen, T.L. (2007) *Ways of Knowing: Competing methodologies in social and political research*. Houndmills, Basingstoke: Palgrave Macmillan.

methodology

Tickner, J.A. (2005) 'What is your research program?: Some feminist answers to international relations methodological questions', *International Studies Quarterly*, 49 (1): 1–21.

van Biezen, I. and Caramani, D. (2006) '(Non) comparative politics in Britain', *Politics*, 26 (1): 29–37.

Narratives

Narratives give us one of the best ways to illustrate how political and social structures operate in any given geographical, societal or cultural context. Narratives are subjective, interpretative representations of events, facts and, more broadly, 'reality'. They allow researchers to explain political behaviour in terms of not only who did what, when and to whom but also address the 'Why?' underlying the behaviour.

Narratives may be thematic, but, more usually, they are chronological. They usually share a cast, a stage and agree on the script (in terms of the events) and 'their defining characteristic is that they explain actions using beliefs and preferences' (Bevir and Rhodes, 2002: 134). Narratives will share some common ground, but, fundamentally, will differ in their interpretations of the terrain.

Narratives are not to be understood as 'truths', but as versions of truths. They may differ in perspective as the stories being told will undoubtedly provide a record of what researchers or writers observe around them. Different narrators see a different 'reality' through their own different lenses, which reflect their own cultural, political and socio-economic understandings. In much the same way that we find contending discourses when using **discourse analysis**, we find competing versions of the same events in narrative accounts because 'The maps, questions and language of each narrative prefigure and encode different historical stories in distinct ways' (Bevir and Rhodes, 2002: 148). How we, as researchers, shape or *frame* our material, then, ultimately affects the outcome of the research material.

Narratives are almost impossible to avoid in the social sciences. If researchers were to present nothing more than their sources and findings in a chronological order, they would provide us with nothing

key research concepts in politics & international relations

more than a 'shopping list' of a series of events and facts. Events provide researchers with their own history and context. These histories are the core of all our research materials as it is how researchers manage and manipulate the events and source material into coherent and convincing accounts that allows us to 'see' something new or place these studies within larger projects of analysis (for example, a Marxist reading of the facts and events).

To illustrate the role of narrative methods, it is helpful to look at two mainstay texts of International Relations: Eric Hobsbawm's *The Age of Extremes* (1994) and E.H. Carr's *The Twenty Years' Crisis, 1919–1939* (2001). Both authors identify key historical events and facts, then set them into thematic patterns in order to indicate a shift in our reading and understanding of twentieth-century politics.

Hobsbawm argues that the twentieth century saw more people killed in war and conflict than ever before, making it the world's bloodiest century of all time. He pinpoints the key events leading to his findings – World War I, the Russian Revolution, the global economic recession, the rise of Nazi Germany leading to World War II, the arms race and the escalation of the Cold War. Most researchers would also take these very same events and historical facts as key points in the century's development. What makes Hobsbawm's research so important and distinct from the work of his peers, however, is the narrative method he uses to 'read' the events – he sets them into a Marxist narrative. Indeed, Marxism is the common, red thread running throughout *The Age of Extremes*. Hobsbawm wants his readers to interpret these key events within a specific theoretical structure, one in which Marxism is regrettably overwhelmed by its opponents. His narrative calls on readers to rethink the historical importance of Marxism and reinvigorate the political process.

Carr reads and frames the same (earlier) twentieth-century events and concerns in a different narrative. His *The Twenty Years' Crisis* places the material in a realist framework and uses this narrative to criticize the liberal internationalist approach to International Relations. His critique rests on what he deems to be its 'idealist' or 'utopian' foundations. He argues that its advocates simply did not see the reality of international politics, but, instead, saw what they wanted to see. They did not see a Hobbesian international system in which states were locked into a brutish competition for power and security. They did not see that this system was anarchical – there was no Leviathan above the states to impose order on inter-state relations. Instead, Carr sees the liberal internationalists as delusional in their view of a rule-obeying international society of states and peoples where there could be cooperation in pursuit of a harmony of all their interests. Carr's realist reading of the early twentieth century reflected his experience and understanding of those same events: his experience at the Paris Peace negotiations after World War I and his interpretation of the global economic recession, the rise of fascism and the new economic order of the USSR.

Although both Hobsbawm and Carr construct and explore similarities, they provide readers with very different stories. It is inevitable that researchers look at the 'real world' and see different things. Indeed, it is the driving force behind social and political research – we see facts and events, read others' views and findings, yet questions may remain.

Narrative methods are part of the interpretivist tradition. All researchers want to convince readers of their work to interpret the political process and global events as they do – to 'sell' their particular narratives over those of others. As students and researchers, then, we have to distinguish between contending narratives and understand that none of these subjectivist accounts constitutes an absolute truth. Carr (1987: 38) himself counselled that 'You cannot fully appreciate the work of a historian unless you have first grasped the standpoint from which he himself approached it; secondly, that that standpoint is itself rooted in a social and historical background'.

FURTHER READING

Bevir, M. and Rhodes, R.A.W. (2002) 'Interpretative theory', in D. Marsh and G. Stoker (eds), *Theory and Methods in Political Science* (2nd edn). Houndmills, Basingstoke: Palgrave Macmillan. pp. 131–52.

Carr, E.H. (1987) *What is History?* (2nd edn). Harmondsworth: Penguin.

Holloway, W. and Jefferson, T. (2000) *Doing Qualitative Research Differently: Free association, narrative and the interview method.* London: Sage.

Moen, T. (2006) 'Reflections on the narrative research approach', *International Journal of Qualitative Methods,* 5 (4); 56–69.

Roberts, G. (2006) 'History, theory and the narrative turn in IR', *Review of International Studies,* 32 (4): 703–14.

EXAMPLES

Autesserre, S. (2012) 'Dangerous tales: dominant narratives on the Congo and their unintended consequences', *African Affairs,* 111(443): 202–22.

Carr, E.H. (2001) *The Twenty Years' Crisis: 1919–1939: An introduction to the study of international relations.* Houndmills, Basingstoke: Palgrave Macmillan.

Hobsbawm, E. (1994) *The Age of Extremes: A history of the world, 1914–1991.* New York: Vintage Books.

Homolar, A. (2010) 'Rebels without a conscience: the evolution of the rogue states narrative in US security policy', *European Journal of International Relations*, 17 (4): 705–27.

Suganami, H. (2008) 'Narrative explanation and international relations: back to basics', *Millennium – Journal of International Studies*, 37 (2): 327–56.

Observation

Observation, in one form or another, lies at the heart of research. In political analysis, researchers are trying to induce or deduce research findings that explain political phenomena, which are usually based on observations of political behaviour.

Observational research can be either structured or unstructured. It can be participant-based or not. The observations may be conducted in an overt or covert way.

Observational research is increasingly referred to as ethnographic research in the social sciences. Ethnographic research originated in anthropology and then migrated into other social sciences, notably sociology, psychology and education.

All variants of ethnographic methods involve what the anthropologist Geertz termed *thick description*. In essence, this is expansive and detailed research notes. The use of thick description allows researchers to provide rich **narratives**, to perhaps highlight an in-depth analysis of a party leadership campaign or a background to an institutional change or policy formation. The object under investigation may not be the main feature of the observation, but the focus will be on developing a tapestry of material about it that will later form the bulk of the narrative, the thick description. For example, a researcher may want to look into the voting patterns of a particular neighbourhood to see if subcultures, prosperity or social forces impact the residents' voting habits. The focus is on interpreting voting behaviour instead of simply describing the situation. It is this very characteristic of **ethnography** as a method that has limited its use by Politics students and academics alike as it takes resources and time whereas many political research projects are limited and an immediate analysis is required in the fast-paced world of politics. Although ethnographic methods are relatively underused in Political Science, they have become somewhat more salient than previously.

Structured observations are common in educational and sociological research in particular. Researchers draw up an observation schedule form and record their observations on it. This schedule has to be devised prior to the observations and be explicit in terms of what to record. The more explicit the schedule, the greater the opportunity for inter- and intra-observer consistency. The resulting data is seen to be systematic and can then be subjected to quantitative analysis.

Structured observations are better at (though not completely) satisfying **validity, reliability** and generalizability criteria than are unstructured observations. Unstructured observations are more of an interpretivist research approach and give rise to more qualitative accounts of behaviour. Such observations are inherently anti-positivist but arguably much better at 'digging down' into the 'whys' of behaviour. The contexts and deeper meanings of activities can be accessed via unstructured observations, especially through participant observations.

Participant observations involve 'deep hanging out' with the subjects, often groups, under observation (Gusterson, 2009: 99). The researchers immerse themselves in the daily lives of the groups they are studying, so they can access the 'nitty-gritty' of that communal life, including the shared meanings and common understandings on which the behaviour is based: 'The researcher studies people in their own space and time, thereby gaining a close and intimate familiarity with them and their practices' (Bray, 2008: 305).

This research method requires that the researchers have strongly developed interpersonal and social skills so they can build the rapport with the subjects that allows such deep access. They also need to be willing to make a significant time commitment to such research projects – McNeill and Chapman (2005: 24) advise that such studies require a minimum of two years. This level of immersion and duration is not only time-costly but also may prove to have costs in terms of the objectivity of the study.

Participant observation, then, is clearly an anti-positivist research method. The aspects seen as strengths by its advocates – not least the deep access to the thoughts and motivations of the subjects – are criticized by its positivist opponents on the grounds of subjectivity.

In participant observation, objectivity may be weakened in two ways. First, the very presence of researchers may alter the behaviour of the subjects because they know they are being watched – the 'Hawthorne effect'. Second, in their aim to build a rapport with the subjects, the researchers might overidentify with them and effectively 'go native', limiting their ability to record and interpret their observations in a more detached way. In participant observation, then, researchers have to perform a fine balancing act. They must become sufficiently involved with the activities and experiences of the subjects to be able to identify communal views, ideas and values, but remain sufficiently removed so that their role as observers is not invalidated.

The 'mechanics' of participant observation also draw criticism from positivists. It is clearly an interpretivist method, as the observers see the behaviour and write up what they have witnessed. The observers need to have regularized their own activities so that their records will be as accurate as possible. It may, however, be impossible for researchers to make contemporaneous records of their observations, so they will need to plan to allow time to do so later. Even if some brief notes are made at the time, however, then, essentially, researchers are recording reconstructions – their perceptions of what they remember to have happened. The accuracy of any interpretivist findings are hard to confirm but those involving memory are more difficult still. Confirmation requires that other methods are used – such as formal or informal **interviewing**, as well as **documentary analysis** – so that the findings can be rendered more reliable. Even then, the issue of replication remains and it may well prove impossible for another researcher to replicate the research findings of a study. This may be because embedded researchers form strong ties and rapport with their groups that are specific to those researchers at that time and in that context.

Participant observation does facilitate inductive research. During their observations, the researchers are able to revise and adapt their research projects, incorporating new dimensions and amending earlier ideas and concepts in light of the subjects' behaviour and their own interactions with them. The flexibility and access of participant observation has led to it being described as 'the difference between sitting in someone's living room with them and peeking in through the keyhole' (Gusterson,

observation

2009: 100). These strengths have led to a growth in ethnographic research into political topics. Originally such methods were deployed in studies of radical political groups and parties, but more recently attention has been given to the role and activities of senior civil servants. Bevir and Rhodes' (2006) non-participant observation study focuses on such individuals, their beliefs and agency within the context of British governance.

Participant observation may be covert – that is, the subjects of the studies are unaware that there are researchers in their midst who are recording their impressions and understandings of the subjects' thoughts, words and actions. The subjects, then, have not given their consent to take part in the studies. This raises obvious ethical considerations for these researchers – even more so if the activities of the group are illegal. The defence for such observation is that, in some exceptional circumstances, a covert approach is essential in order to gain access to a specific field of study and/or to protect researchers in the field.

FURTHER READING

Bray, Z. (2008) 'Ethnographic approaches', in D. della Porta and M. Keating (eds), *Approaches and Methodologies in the Social Sciences: A pluralist perspective*. Cambridge: Cambridge University Press. pp. 296–315.

Gusterson, H. (2009) 'Ethnographic research', in A. Klotz and D. Prakash (eds), *Qualitative Methods in International Relations: A pluralist guide*. Houndmills, Basingstoke: Palgrave Macmillan. pp. 93–113.

McNeill, P. and Chapman, S. (2005) *Research Methods* (3rd edn). Abingdon: Routledge.

Moug, P. (2007) 'Non-participative observation in political research: the "poor" relation?', *Politics*, 27 (2): 108–14.

EXAMPLES

Bevir, M. and Rhodes, R.A.W. (2006) *Governance Stories*. Abingdon: Routledge.

Clarke, A., Holland, C., Katz, J. and Peace, S. (2009) 'Learning to see: Lessons from a participatory observation research project in public spaces', *International Journal of Social Research Methodology*, 12 (4): 345–60.

Geertz, C. (1973) 'Thick description: toward an interpretive theory of culture'. In *The Interpretation of Cultures: Selected Essays*. New York: Basic Books. pp. 3–30.

Glazer, J.M. (1996) 'The challenge of campaign watching: Seven lessons of participant–observation research', *PS: Political Science and Politics*, 29 (3): 533–7.

Pearson, G. (2009) 'The researcher as hooligan: Where "participant" observation means breaking the law', *International Journal of Social Research Methodology*, 12 (3): 243–55.

key research concepts in politics & international relations

While information created by governmental agencies can provide a wealth of useful information for students of Politics and International Relations, there are some considerations that may affect its 'usefulness' for research purposes. When dealing with official data, we can distinguish between quantitative and qualitative sources –both types are affected by different research considerations. An important issue to consider is access. Much official information can be classified as either *closed access*, such as government documents covered by the Official Secrets Act, or *restricted access*, such as British Royal papers, which are accessible only to the monarch (May, 1997: 159–62).

Although the term 'official statistics' may imply the sense of a monolithic collection of data (or systematic set), the overall collection, production, maintenance and dissemination of the information through governmental channels can be variable. The methods of data collection, the amount of centralized control, the methods of compilation and the number of involved agencies can vary from one data set to the next. Some statistics can be gathered from local government councils and distributed to other similar bodies, while other statistics can be gathered locally but released at higher levels and include regional or administrative levels. Yet other statistics are derived from national figures (census polling) and systematically collated, reviewed, managed and distributed from central agencies.

Official statistics cover themes such as the economy, the labour market, welfare, populations and migration and are crucial for contemporary research, partly because of their volume and depth. Examples include the ten-year census (collected since 1801), the Labour Force Survey (collected since 1973) and the British Crime Survey (collected since 1982). Official statistics are particularly important for our understanding of *demographics* – that is, patterns of stability and change in the study of human populations. The Office for National Statistics (ONS) produces a vast wealth of data, most of which receives very little publicity and attracts minimal public interest. However, being unable to scrutinize the raw data means that aggregate data can hide biases because it is not apparent exactly *how* the trends have been calculated.

official data

95

Traditionally, statistical information was generated by the UK government with the intention of operationalizing comparative analyses of social development and change. However, this has been undermined by the changing 'mode, regularity and timing of publications' (Tant, 1995: 255). Tant's underlying concern is not only that data is being manipulated for political gain but also it is, after all, public information increasingly governed by 'political subjectivity' and kept hidden. In 2005, the then Chancellor of the Exchequer, Gordon Brown, announced that the ONS would be given independence from government to restore confidence in national statistics.

The Government Statisticians' Collective (GSC) has identified four main ways in which data may be manipulated:

- Changing definitions of terms – this hinders the **reliability** of comparisons made over time. Cloke et al. (2001: 259) argue that a case study of homelessness and, more specifically, those identified as 'rough sleepers', can illustrate 'the power of numbers in discourses relating to homelessness in Britain'. Rough sleepers are only one way in which homelessness can be measured as this concept lacks a universally accepted definition, but such figures are used in determining policy 'solutions' to perceived 'problems'. A central concern is that, whatever measurement is used, it will underestimate the total extent of homelessness and a rough sleeper method of enumeration contributes towards rendering homelessness invisible in rural areas – it is more noticeable in inner cities. For Cloke et al., the nature and scale of problems can be distorted and obscured by a tendency to give credit to statistical facts or 'knowledge'.
- The 'unjustifiable extrapolation of trends' – by manipulating the parameters of the time periods studied, governments can ensure data is as favourable as possible.
- The manipulation of adjustments by turning data from raw into adjusted figures – that is, taking into account some form of context, such as, 'seasonally adjusted' unemployment figures. The Office of National Statistics records unemployment data in non-seasonally adjusted and seasonally adjusted formats. The present seasonally adjusted claimant count series goes back to 1971 and is adjusted to allow for significant changes to benefit rules.
- The manipulation of categories – by making age groups smaller or larger, putting certain figures into a general category entitled 'other' or 'miscellaneous'. It is well documented that the government

altered the way in which unemployment was officially measured in the UK in the 1980s over 30 times. Vigderhous (1978) writes of the challenge of comparing crime rates as many forms of criminal behaviour are culturally specific and subject to different definitions. This may be seen in the almost annual furore over crime statistics – specifically, perceived discrepancies between those of the British Crime Survey and those recorded by the different police forces within the UK.

Political researchers may have become more optimistic thanks to the implementation of the Freedom of Information Act 2000 in the UK, which came into effect in 2005. The Act allows individuals to request data from any public authority (therefore covering central and local government), though a range of exemptions apply (predominantly relating to appropriateness of cost or a public interest defence). Murray (2011) highlights this development as being a quick and efficient gateway to data – no tricky gatekeepers, no fieldwork, travel or transcription costs. This said, access does not resolve the thornier concerns of reliability and accuracy.

FURTHER READING

Levitas, R. and Guy, W. (eds) (1996) *Interpreting Official Statistics*. London: Routledge.
May, T. (1997) *Social Research: Issues, methods, process* (2nd edn). Buckingham: Open University Press.
Murray, C. (2011) 'Using the UK Freedom of Information Act for research', *MethodsNews*, Newsletter from the ESRC National Centre for Research Methods, p. 6. Also available online at: http://eprints.ncrm.ac.uk/2042/7/MethodsNews_Winter2011.pdf (accessed 11 September 2012).

EXAMPLES

Cloke, P., Milbourne, P. and Widdowfield, R. (2001) 'Making the homeless count?: Enumerating rough sleepers and the distortion of homelessness', *Policy & Politics*, 29 (3): 259–79.
Government Statisticians' Collective (1993) 'How official statistics are produced: Views from the inside', in M. Hammersley (ed.), *Social Research: Philosophy, politics and practice*. London: Sage.
Tant, A. (1995) 'The politics of official statistics', *Government and Opposition*, 30 (2): 254–66.
Vigderhous, G. (1978) 'Methodological problems confronting cross-cultural criminological research using official data', *Human Relations*, 31 (3): 229–47.

official data

Simply stated, ontology is about explaining what can be examined via research and examining the nature of the social and political world. It is a branch of philosophy that is concerned with reality and 'what exists'. It is differentiated from **epistemology**, which is concerned with how we know what exists.

An ontology, therefore, is a **theory** of 'being' that is concerned with the impact of essential differences (such as gender, race). Some of the American Right, for example, have attempted to argue that poverty is linked to race – a foundationalist claim. An anti-foundationalist claim places emphasis on the social construction of phenomena – that is, certain ethnic groups may be more likely to suffer poverty because they have less access to good education, career opportunities, networks and so on rather than because of their ethnicity. Similar arguments are put forward to explain the dominance of men in most positions of political power. The question becomes, is this because politics is natural for men or because opportunities, attitudes, norms and so on have tended to be more encouraging to men than women in this area? Therefore, our ontological position is our view 'about the nature of the world' (Marsh and Furlong, 2002: 18). Formally, ontology is the statement of a logical theory.

As a political researcher, you need to have particular ideas concerning the basic ontological questions relating to your studies. For example, 'What is politics?' Is it the collection of events, the writings about and analysis of these events or both? If the approach is focused on a *critical reading* of politics, the ontological questions would refer to a 'virtual' reality that is shaped by cultural, social, economic, political, gender values and ethnic histories and so on. These readings of political events, for example, allow researchers to discover a broader analytical field. That is, ontology works as a description of the concepts and relationships that *can* exist for a political actor or a political community. Ontology also informs the language and position of the argument and analysis that follows. For traditional International Relations (IR), what 'exists' is that which can be represented – that which is real.

In the political sense, ontology allows researchers to address the basic questions and outline the subject, a relationship and an object to analyse.

Political studies (including International Relations) often utilize one of the four main ontological methods:

- empiricism – arguing that we can observe the world and evaluate those observations in relation to existing facts
- **realism** – the idea that unknown facts exist waiting to be discovered
- **positivism** – focusing on the researchers' observations and how they deduce the facts
- postmodernism – which holds that facts are fluid and elusive, so we should focus only on our observational claims.

There has been a series of 'Great Debates' in International Relations focusing on the ontological assumptions of different perspectives. The first such debate between idealist and realist approaches focused on their contending views on the drivers of state behaviour and how security could best be provided within international systems or society. Realism won out as its core assumptions – an anarchical international system resembling a Hobbesian environment in which states must help themselves to security and wherein the balance of power is the best mechanism for reducing conflict – seemed to be borne out by the reality of superpower competition in the early Cold War system.

The second such debate took place between traditionalists and **behaviouralists** and was chiefly about what ought to be the focus of study in International Relations – the behaviour of the various actors, scientifically and systematically defined and measured or the dominant or pseudo-scientific unreliable interpretations ascribed to their actions. The behaviouralists triumphed in this debate and, as Brown and Ainley (2009: 32) note, their legacy is still visible in the subject area as 'a methodology that essentially reflected this [behaviouralist] training took hold and has not yet weakened its grip'.

The third debate was the 'neo-neo debate' between neorealists and neoliberals, which was not quite as profound as its predecessors. These two approaches share a number of assumptions – the anarchical nature of the international system and the rationality of states, for example – as well as being disposed towards **rational choice** theories. It is this shared acceptance of the validity of a positivist approach towards understanding International Relations that has been challenged by post-positivists in the most recent debate.

Marxists, constructivists and a wide array of critical theorists have rejected the dominant positivist account of International Relations.

ontology

99

Their work has brought in a variety of other issues and processes for consideration – and the various post-positivist approaches have their own distinct ontological foundations that guide their differing research agendas.

As students of International Relations, you will encounter these different approaches and their respective ontologies and, in so doing, perhaps come to appreciate that there is no 'right' answer in this vibrant field of study.

FURTHER READING

Brown, C. and Ainley, K. (2009) *Understanding International Relations* (4th edn). Houndmills, Basingstoke: Palgrave Macmillan.

Burnham, P., Gilland Lutz, K., Grant, W. and Layton-Henry, Z. (2004) *Research Methods in Politics*. Houndmills, Basingstoke: Palgrave Macmillan.

Jørgensen, K.E. (2010) *International Relations Theory: A new introduction*. Houndmills, Basingstoke: Palgrave Macmillan.

Marsh, D. and Furlong, P. (2002) 'A skin not a sweater: Ontology and epistemology in political science', in D. Marsh and G. Stoker (eds), *Theory and Methods in Political Science* (2nd edn). Houndmills, Basingstoke: Palgrave Macmillan.

Moses, J.W. and Knutsen, T.L. (2007) *Ways of Knowing: Competing methodologies in social and political research*. Houndmills, Basingstoke: Palgrave Macmillan.

Seale, C. (2004) *Researching Society and Culture*. London: Sage.

EXAMPLES

Finnemore, M. and Sikkink, K. (2001) 'Taking stock: The constructivist research program in international relations and comparative politics', *Annual Review of Political Science*, 4: 391–416.

Jackson, P.T. (2008) 'Foregrounding ontology: Dualism, monism, and international relations theory', *Review of International Studies*, 34 (1): 129–53.

Patomäki, H. (2001) 'The challenge of critical theories: Peace research at the start of the new century', *Journal of Peace Research*, 38 (6): 723–37.

Patomäki, H. and Wright, C. (2000) 'After post-positivism: The promises of critical realism', *International Studies Quarterly*, 44 (2): 213–37.

Price, R. and Reus-Smit, C. (1998) 'Dangerous liaisons?: Critical international theory and constructivism', *European Journal of International Relations*, 4 (3): 259–94.

Sterling-Folker, J. (2002) 'Realism and the constructivist challenges: Rejecting, reconstructing, or rereading', *International Studies Review*, 4 (1): 73–97.

Wendt, A. (1992) 'Anarchy is what states make of it: The social construction of power politics', *International Organization*, 46 (2): 391–425.

Essentially, a paradigm is a framework on which there is a common agreement. While it is not restricted to the area of research methods, we can see by examining dominant research approaches (such as **behaviouralism** and **rational choice**) that there are common principles of acceptable **methodology**.

Kuhn (1970: 173) defines a paradigm as 'the entire constellation of beliefs, values, techniques and so on shared by the members of a given community.' The techniques aspect relates to a consensus regarding what is appropriate research methodology. In this environment, Kuhn claimed that 'normal science' could be progressed. Researchers and practitioners would study within this common framework, studying their specific areas of interest using commonly accepted methods and presenting their respective findings for peer review. Thus, research would tick along nicely, methods and outcomes would be interrogated and progress would be verified.

Nothing lasts forever, though, and it was envisaged that there would come a time when this collegial environment and its prevailing orthodoxy would be challenged through a revolution. The dominant paradigm would be challenged when a scientist reached conclusions that could not be reconciled with the commonly accepted thinking and wisdom of the day. Copernicus' heliocentric theory that put the Sun rather than the Earth at the centre of the universe is a clear case in point. As more and more questions are raised about the **validity** of the dominant paradigm, as more and more research findings cannot be accommodated within its premises, then there occurs a scientific revolution and an accompanying paradigm shift (Kuhn, 1970: 6):

> the profession can no longer evade anomalies that subvert the existing tradition of scientific practice – then beginning the extraordinary investigations that lead the profession at last to a new set of commitments, a new basis for the practice of science.

However, other scholars, such as Gorard (2003), warn against the paradigm 'prison', which is when researchers feel that they must stay allied to a positivist or realist philosophy. This 'prison' is explored by Blaug (1999: 34, 43) in his critique of the privileging of a hierarchical organizational paradigm in mainstream Political Science – an oversight that neglects the significance of anti-institutional and disorganized political forms:

> Modern, Western, male political science meditates upon, and almost exclusively upon, hierarchical activity. It is a science largely about elites. Whether right or left wing in one's political orientation, alternative political forms are thus seen to be obviously ineffective, or insufficiently hierarchical.

Similarly, Davis (2003) critiques the elite–mass paradigm within media studies, instead arguing that the concept of mass influence is no longer sufficient to explain unequal power relations across society. By **interviewing** elite actors drawn from political communications in the UK, Davis challenges the paradigm that elites seek only to influence the masses by suggesting an elite–elite communications network is equally important: 'public mediated debate on significant issues and decisions is declining. Conversely, private debate between powerful elites about public issues has become all the more important' (Davis, 2003: 684).

The progression from a restrictive paradigm is seen in the quantitative versus qualitative debate. While many political researchers may still tend towards particular types of data, there is a greater acceptance of – indeed, support for – a **triangulation** of data collection methods. We also need to be careful when we read academic papers that claim to be paradigmatic in their impact because 'Paradigm formation must be anchored by a major scientific achievement that a particular community of scientists finds convincing' (Walker, 2010: 435). Accommodating more interpretivist approaches and methods within research does not undermine the need for robust research findings, the soundness and value of which is accepted by a community of peers.

FURTHER READING

della Porta, D. and Keating, M. (2008) 'How many approaches in the social sciences?: An epistemological introduction', in D. della Porta and M. Keating, *Approaches and Methodologies in the Social Sciences: A pluralist perspective*. Cambridge: Cambridge University Press. pp. 19–39.

Gliner, J.A. and Morgan, G.A. (2000) 'A tale of two paradigms: Quantitative and qualitative', in J.A. Gliner and G.A. Morgan, *Research Methods in Applied Settings: An integrated approach to design and analysis*. Mahwah, NJ: Lawrence Erlbaum. pp. 15–30.

Gorard, S. (2003) *Quantitative Methods in Social Science*. London: Continuum.

Kuhn, T. (1970) *The Structure of Scientific Revolutions*. Chicago, IL: University of Chicago Press.

Walker, T.C. (2010) 'The perils of paradigm mentalities: Revisiting Kuhn, Laktos, and Popper', *Perspectives on Politics*, 8 (2): 433–51.

EXAMPLES

Blaug, R. (1999) 'The tyranny of the visible: Problems in the evaluation of anti-institutional radicalism', *Organization*, 6 (1): 33–56.

Bosse, G. (2012) 'A partnership with dictatorship: Explaining the paradigm shift in European Union policy towards Belarus', *Journal of Common Market Studies*, 50 (3): 367–84.

Davis, A. (2003) 'Whither mass media and power?: Evidence for a critical elite theory alternative', *Media, Culture & Society*, 25 (5): 669–90.

Lane, D. (1997) 'Transition under Yeltsin: The nomenklatura and political elite circulation', *Political Studies*, 45 (5): 855–74.

McAllister, L. (2001) 'Gender, nation and party: An uneasy alliance for Welsh nationalism', *Women's History Review*, 10 (1): 51–70.

Mü, D. (2011) 'From pragmatism to dogmatism: European Union governance, policy paradigms, and financial regulation', *New Political Economy*, 16 (2): 185–206.

Paris, R. (2001) 'Human security: Paradigm shift or hot air?', *International Security*, 26 (2): 87–102.

Sterling-Folker, J. (2000) 'Competing paradigms or birds of a feather?: Constructivism and neoliberal institutionalism compared', *International Studies Quarterly*, 44 (1): 97–119.

Rushton, S. and Williams, O.D. (2012) 'Frames, paradigms and power: Global health policy-making under neo-liberalism', *Global Society*, 26 (2): 147–67.

positivism

Positivism

Politics and International Relations as disciplines have been dominated by positivism, which has involved a commitment to the adoption of the methodologies used in the natural sciences to explain the social world. When looked at in this light the inter-**paradigm** debate of IR between idealism, **realism** and structuralism begins to look narrow as all these paradigms are constructed under positivist assumptions. Comte, the nineteenth-century French philosopher who was the first to coin not only the term 'positivism' but also 'sociology', saw positivism as a 'science of society' based on the methods of the natural sciences, namely the tried and tested **observation**.

During the 1920s, logical positivism – which made the radical claim that science is the only true form of knowledge – fed into the social sciences. By making this claim, logical positivists argued that moral statements and value judgements were meaningless because they could not be verified or falsified by experience or observation. Another variant of positivism came out of logical positivism but separated itself from its predecessor by disputing what counts as knowledge.

The underlying assumptions are:

- facts and value judgements are distinct from each other
- empirical validation or falsification is the basis for explaining the 'real' world
- regularities exist in both the social and natural worlds
- the unity of science, including the social.

Taking account of these four assumptions, we can define positivism as a methodological view that combines naturalism and a belief in regular, consistent occurrences. It is qualified by empirically charged **epistemology** that, in turn, is committed to an objectivism about the interrelationship between evidence and knowledge.

As any student will learn while studying Politics, defining terminology includes positioning the concept or method in the ongoing debates. With positivism come questions as to its limitations and weaknesses. The positivist (or empirical) epistemology is based on the view that the only sustainable arguments for justified reality are those which rest on observation. This view offers a very narrow epistemology, as everything has to be based on direct observation. A second criticism comes from the belief that pure perception (objective viewpoint) is simply impossible. There can be no purely 'objective' observations as we each view the world from our own positions.

Positivism is sometimes equated with **behaviouralism**, becoming regarded as having a limited reliance on quantitative data and, thus, disregarding the experience and development of actors as actual knowledge. Furthermore, although empiricism and positivism are often argued to be the same thing, the reality is not so clear-cut. Positivism is actually a methodological approach with an empiricist epistemology.

Even given these questions and limitations, positivism has had a dominant influence on the development of Politics and International Relations as disciplines in so far as it has influenced what they could cover and explore. If we take the reflective theories of International Relations – critical theory, postmodernism, some **feminism** and constructivism – and look at their commonalities, what we find is that they all share just one thing: an aversion to the scientific world of positivism. Looking back to the debates of the 1970s and 1980s in these disciplines, they were focused on the nature and structure of international relations, particularly the age-old belief in there being a distinct barrier between the international and the national as it was then seen as eroding away. The two political *worlds* were merging, each being faced with challenges traditionally seen to belong to the other. Most importantly for international relations, state borders, the sovereignty of the states, were becoming permeable. No longer was the primary focus on the relationships between states, but, instead, a developed concentration on movement across states. This redirected focus, led by the pluralists, was seen as an attack on the overly simplistic 'billiard ball' metaphor of realism. This metaphor stressed that states were the only actors worthy of attention in international politics. Each state was regarded as atomistic and egotistical, driven relentlessly by the urge to increase its power relative to that of the other states. The more power that the state attained, the less there was for its competitor states in this zero-sum world. The pluralists rejected this static and parsimonious view of international politics, on the grounds that it failed completely to accommodate the complexities of the modern international world.

In the groundbreaking *Power and Interdependence*, Keohane and Nye (2001) depicted a version of the international system built on complex interdependent units that emphasized transnationalism and multi-level connections as being global forces. The pluralists asserted it was these global forces that played major roles in the liberal world order of modern international relations. Fukuyama's (1992) *The End of History and the Last Man*, on the breakdown of the Soviet Union, also gave pluralism a permanent role in the discipline.

When looking at the continuing relevance of realism within international relations, it can be seen that positivism is still dominant, though there remains a disagreement about what ought to count as positivism in international relations. Some scholars identify it with realism alone, but pluralism, in its neoliberal strand, for example, remains broadly positivist. To conflate realism with positivism is to misunderstand that realism is a **theory** of *how* the world works and positivism is an epistemology describing how to investigate the world we find around us.

The positivists' belief that the international system contains a 'knowable reality' which is revealed by a theoretical approach is important because it gives International Relations theory a method, but also because its empiricist epistemology has highlighted what *could* be studied and what kinds of actors and processes exist in international relations.

FURTHER READING

Comte, A. (1974) *Discourse on the Positive Spirit*. London: Heinemann.
Friedman, M. (1999) *Reconsidering Logical Positivism*. Cambridge: Cambridge University Press.
Fukuyama, F. (1992) *The End of History and the Last Man*. New York: Avon Books.
Keohane, R. and Nye, J. (2001) *Power and Interdependence* (3rd edn). New York: Longman.
Reisch, G. (2005) *How the Cold War Transformed Philosophy of Science: To the icy slopes of logic*. New York: Cambridge University Press.

EXAMPLES

Kurki, M. (2011) 'The limitations of the critical edge: Reflections on critical and philosophical IR scholarship today', *Millennium: Journal of International Studies*, 40 (1): 129–46.
Sanders, D. (2002) 'Behaviouralism', in D. Marsh and G. Stoker (eds), *Theory and Methods in Political Science* (2nd edn). Houndmills, Basingstoke: Palgrave Macmillan.
Turner, J.H. (2006) 'Explaining the social world: Historicism versus positivism', *The Sociological Quarterly*, 47 (3): 451–63.

Post-positivism

Post-positivism came out of the attempt in the 1960s by some scholars – Kuhn being one of the leading lights of the post-positivist revolution – to understand and *reflect* on the world around them, questioning and exploring issues, concepts and strategies that most saw as permanent features of politics, such as states have borders, governments rule the people.

Kuhn's understanding of science varied greatly from that of the positivists. Whereas they were interested in the analysis of knowledge, Kuhn focused on the historical development of the subject. Essentially, Kuhn was challenging the positivists' analysis and its outcomes that were, in part, normative and prescriptive. So, whereas the positivists were only interested in the rationality of concepts, arguments and theories but not their empirical description, Kuhn was interested (so it seemed) in the explanation and description of how science functions and how it develops. He was not concerned with prescribing how best 'to do' research.

During the 1980s, a theoretical shift developed, moving away from the debate concerning the variety of positivist positions (traditionally, in International Relations, referred to as the inter**paradigm** debate) and towards one on the nature of political and social enquiry itself. The debate can be summed up as a defence of **positivism**. The shift occurred as scholars were attempting to 'understand' the political world and its processes rather than 'explain' them.

Neorealism and neoliberalism applied the logic of rationalist economic theories to International Relations, but both reached different conclusions. Reflectivists (another term for the post-positivists) challenged the neorealists' and neoliberals' (collectively termed the rationalists or **positivists**) **methodological, ontological, epistemological** and normative assumptions. From then onwards, post-positivism entered the evolving debates on the 'real world'. By questioning the positivist approaches to knowledge and challenging the *scientific* method, post-positivism initially focused on concerns relating to understanding the foundations of dominant discourses in Politics and International Relations. Due to the nature of those challenges, which queried the very foundations on which positivism is based, the post-postivists' theoretical arguments were labelled critical theory.

One of the key points to raise here is that post-positivism was not actually an attempt to show that the positivists' logic was wrong. The developments in politics, science and philosophy were happening quickly. Some criticisms were not focused on positivism alone, but aimed more broadly at modern understanding of the world and our role in it (in general, an attack on modernism). This *new* way of understanding the world became known as postmodernism.

It is important to note that postmodernism has, in part, assimilated post-positivism, in so far as it claims Kuhn and others are postmodernists. As a result the term post-positivism, although still used to a certain extent in International Relations, predominantly fell out of fashion in the mid-1980s. One of the problems with this merging or assimilating is that the prefix 'post' has lost some of its former precise reflection and focus on positivism and is now very vague in meaning, to the point that it is now criticized for its boundaries being blurred. There is no doubt that postmodernism is applied to different and sometimes incoherent views and arguments.

From an International Relations perspective, we can say that the modern Westphalian system was supposed to be progressive, promising to liberate humankind from the irrationality and ignorance of their medieval and feudal pasts. Postmodernists, however, base their opposition to modernism on an analysis of the modern world's record. For example, over questions of morality, postmodernists could well query whether the modernist approach has been a force for liberation or a source of repression and subjugation, with its imposed morality.

Most conventional International Relations theories can be placed within the modern framework. One clear example is neorealism, which is grounded in the structure of the modernist (Westphalian) international system. By linking its **theory** to this particular period in history neorealism is practically incapable of an evolution in historical terms.

Neoliberalism, an even more recent pluralist account of International Relations, can be criticized for being boxed within the Westphalian image of the world. Despite being more open to alternatives, such as the declining power of sovereignty, neoliberals remain bounded to the state, in so far as they have failed to find an appropriate replacement for it.

Post-positivism, then, focuses on what positivist assumptions have taken for granted or neglected. As a methodology, it does not seek to improve the social sciences but, instead, to make explicit their underlying assumptions and foundations. Positivist, empiricist and logical and rational assumptions dominate the social sciences, yet they have been accused of failing to deliver results when it comes to political and social issues. Post-positivists argue that traditional theories and methods have been covering up abuses in democratic societies and working to sustain totalitarian states.

FURTHER READING

Edkins, J. and Vaughan-Williams, N. (2009) *Critical Theorists and International Relations*. Abingdon: Routledge.

Groff, R. (2004) *Critical Realism, Post-positivism and the Possibility of Knowledge*. Abingdon: Routledge.

Jones, R.W. (2001) *Critical Theory and International Relations*. Boulder, CO: Lynne Rienner.

Kuhn, T. (1977) *The Essential Tension*. Chicago, IL: University of Chicago Press.

Kuhn, T. (1996) *The Structure of Scientific Revolutions* (3rd edn). Chicago, IL: University of Chicago Press.

Smith, S., Booth, K. and Zalewski, M. (eds) (1996) *International Theory: Positivism and beyond*. Cambridge: Cambridge University Press.

EXAMPLES

Ackerly, B., Stern, M. and True, J. (2006) *Feminist Methodologies for International Relations*. Cambridge: Cambridge University Press.

Finnemore, M. and Sikkink, K. (2001) 'Taking stock: The constructivist research program in international relations and comparative politics', *Annual Review of Political Science*, 4: 391–416.

Michel, T. (2012) 'In Heidegger's shadow: A phenomenological critique of critical realism', *Review of International Studies*, 38 (1): 209–22.

Patomaki, H. and Wight, C. (2000) 'After post-positivism: The promises of critical realism', *International Studies Quarterly*, 44 (2): 213–37.

Presenting Quantitative Analysis

An important skill that students do well to develop is presenting quantitative data correctly. The developments in analytical software, such as Excel and SPSS, have made this a much easier task than it once was. This said, students sometimes struggle to present an evaluation of quantitative data in a clear and succinctly explained manner. A common error is to expect 'the data to explain themselves' – tables and graphs being inserted without any attempt to explain what they demonstrate. To this end, it is crucial that all tables and graphs are appropriately titled. How precisely data is best presented depends on what we want to show and how many variables there are.

USING TABLES

Univariate analysis is the explanation of a single variable. Often, for example, frequency is presented in two ways – as the number of occurrences (which is referred to as *n*) and as a percentage of all cases. The latter is particularly useful when dealing with large numbers of cases.

Once we move on to analysing multiple variables, cross-tabulations are used to create contingency tables. This assists in identifying relationships between **variables**. When creating a contingency table, it is important that the variables are calculated in the correct way – the independent variable should be the column variable and the dependent variable the row variable (see **levels of measurement** for information on which test to use).

Table 2 Women MPs elected to the UK's House of Commons

Election year	1979	1997	2001	2010
Number (n)	19	120	118	143
Percentage of MPs	3	18.2	17.9	22

Table 3 Westminster parliamentary constituencies with the greatest percentage increase in parliamentary electors in the year to December 2011

Rank	Parliamentary constituency	County (C) or borough (B)	Total parliamentary electorate (thousands) December 2010	December 2011	Percentage change 2010–2011
1	Newcastle upon Tyne East	B	65.2	68.9	5.7
2	Aberdeen North	B	64.8	67.5	4.2
3	Nottingham South	B	69.2	72.0	4.1
4	Ceredigion	C	56.0	58.3	4.1
5	Nottingham East	B	59.5	61.9	4.0
6	Blackley and Broughton	B	69.0	71.5	3.7
7	Berwick-upon-Tweed	C	55.8	57.7	3.5
8	Maidstone and The Weald	C	70.6	73.0	3.4
9	Sutton and Cheam	B	66.6	68.8	3.3
10	Milton Keynes North	C	81.2	83.9	3.3

Source: Office for National Statistics, National Records of Scotland, Electoral Office for Northern Ireland

USING DIAGRAMS

The advantage of using statistical packages such as Excel and SPSS is that not only do they generate frequency tables but they also enable the creation of charts and graphs. This lets us easily see the relative sizes of the different categories. This is achieved in a variety of ways. In univariate analysis, the following are used:

- pie charts – useful for showing information such as vote shares in an election

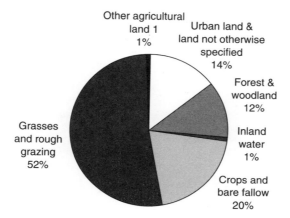

Figure 1   Land use 2008 United Kingdom

Source: Office of National Statistics, 7 November 2012

Jawed Khan and Kahwei Hoo 'Measuring National Well-being – The Natural Environment' www.ons.gov.uk/ons/dcp171766_286230.pdf

- bar charts and histograms – the former are employed for nominal and ordinal variables, the latter for interval/ratio variables

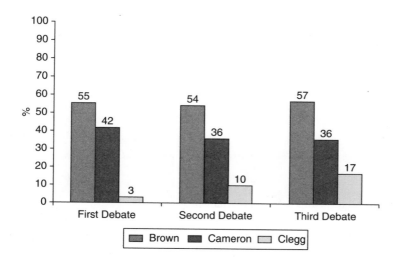

Figure 2   Who did the worst job in party leader debates

Source: The British Election Study [http://bes.utdallas.edu/2009/]

- line graphs – these are particularly useful for illustrating trends over time. They are commonly used for illustrating electoral turnout trends or political leadership popularity.

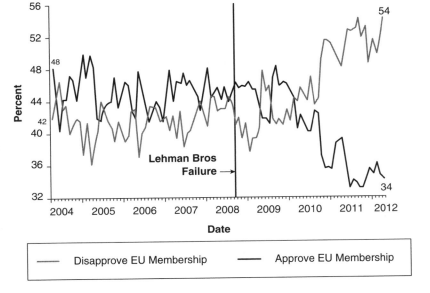

Figure 3   Increasing Euro-skepticism: attitudes towards British Membership in the EU

Source: The British Election Study [http://bes.utdallas.edu/2009/]

In bivariate analysis, scatter diagrams can be used to plot the relationship between two interval/ratio variables. This enables us to see whether there is:

- no relationship between variables
- a positive relationship – that is, the variables increase at a similar rate, so, for example, as people become more interested in politics, the likelihood that they will vote also increases

key research concepts in
politics & international relations

- a negative relationship – that is, as one variable increases, the other decreases, so, for example, as political corruption increases, political trust declines.

FURTHER READING

Bryman, A. (2004) *Social Research Methods* (2nd edn). Oxford: Oxford University Press. Chapter 11.

Burnham, P., Gilland Lutz, K., Grant, W. and Layton-Henry, Z. (2008) *Research Methods in Politics* (2nd edn). Houndmills, Basingstoke: Palgrave Macmillan. Chapter 5.

Manheim, J.B., Rich, R.C., Willnat, L. and Brians, C.L. (2008) *Empirical Political Analysis* (7th edn). Harlow: Pearson. Chapter 15.

EXAMPLES

Curtice, J. and Heath, O. (2012), 'Does choice deliver? Public satisfaction with the health service', *Political Studies*, 60: 484–503.

Evans, E. and Harrison, L. (2012) 'Candidate selection in British second order elections: A comparison of electoral system and party strategy effects', *The Journal of Legislative Studies*, 18 (2): 242–60.

Langlois, J.-P. P and Langlois, C.C. (2012) 'Does the principle of convergence really hold? War, uncertainty and the failure of bargaining', *British Journal of Political Science*, 42 (3): 511–36.

Primary Sources

A question often asked by those who are new to the process of political research is what is the distinction between primary and secondary levels of analysis? Generally speaking, undergraduate students would not be expected to generate and analyse substantive primary data. In order to address issues surrounding **reliability** and **validity**, students would simply not have access to the basic resources necessary for data creation. In contrast, doctoral students are expected to conduct a 'substantial piece of original research'. Though it is sometimes incorrectly assumed that this entails creating new data, it is not necessarily the case. For example, the British Election Study (BES) involves the creation of a new set of data during a British General Election, which then acts as a primary resource for a whole range of electoral researchers – often with the intention of tracking trends over time. In the process of writing their undergraduate dissertations, students would typically read and cite these researchers in order to make claims about electoral trends in the UK. These researchers' published articles and texts are a secondary source based on primary data.

The importance of primary resources is often emphasized by International Relations researchers who prioritize a historical approach (Moses and Knutsen, 2007: 120–1):

> Primary sources are the direct outcomes of historical events and experiences. They include eyewitness accounts (for example, interviews and oral histories), original documents (for example, diaries and school records), and diplomatic reports (for example, the original assessment and papers given to decision makers, papers and minutes from committee meetings) …

As such, the distinction between primary and secondary sources often centres on the extent to which something is trustworthy (see **documentary analysis**). In attempting to develop a greater understanding of the European Union's foreign policy towards the 'Mediterranean', Pace (2002) utilized a triangulated methods approach that incorporated **discourse analysis** of EU primary sources and interviews with members of the European Commission. What Pace's analysis of the primary documentary sources revealed was that the EU Commission suffers an inconsistency in its various references to the area depicted as 'Mediterranean'.

For political researchers, many primary sources will be deposited in archives. For example, the Churchill Archives Centre, based at Churchill College, Cambridge, is host to over 570 collections of personal papers and archives documenting the history of the Churchill era and after, as well as many files from Margaret Thatcher's private archive. The Clinton Presidential Library and Museum at Little Rock, Arkansas, contains many official documents. Not all primary sources take the form of documents. Data sets have been mentioned, but, of course, audio and visual recordings may be included.

Yet, we should not assume that all public figures have assiduously saved and archived their letters, memoirs and speeches. Indeed, the differential application of Freedom of Information laws means that many political documents are subject to restricted access – at least for a substantive period of time – in the interests of 'public security'. The same tends not to apply to large-scale quantitative data sets as they are likely to 'anonymize' those who are studied.

A criticism of the preference for primary sources in historical research is that it privileges certain political views. We should ask questions about why someone chooses to methodically record their thoughts and the conversations of others and why some primary sources survive and are archived for the benefit of researchers while others' voices remain 'silent' (Moses and Knutsen, 2007: 198):

> kings, generals and MPs are more likely to leave primary accounts than are housewives, gravediggers, fishermen, bakers and mimes.

An example of 'what is recorded and survives' is the case of Mathilde Hanzel-Hübner – a nineteenth-century Viennese schoolteacher and 'life-long feminist activist' whose name was reported differently in different sources. Bernold and Gehmacher (1999: 238) refer to the production, in the words of Bourdieu, of a 'biographical illusion'. Indeed, the story of this activist only came to public light when private papers were given to the University of Vienna to facilitate an exhibition on women's suffrage.

FURTHER READING

Moses, J.W. and Knutsen, T.L. (2007) *Ways of Knowing: Competing methodologies in social and political research*. Houndmills, Basingstoke: Palgrave Macmillan.

EXAMPLES

Bernold, M. and Gehmacher, J. (1999) 'A private eye on feminist agency: Reflections on self-documentation, biography, and political consciousness', *Women's Studies International Forum*, 22 (2): 237–47.
Pace, M. (2002) 'The ugly duckling of Europe: The Mediterranean in the foreign policy of the European Union', *Journal of Contemporary European Studies*, 10 (2): 189–210.

primary sources

It has long been a tradition with social and political science to differentiate between quantitative and qualitative methods, and there are clearly research hypotheses that can be addressed in different ways, depending on the preferred methodological approach. We should not assume, however, that researchers can only engage with qualitative *or* **quantitative methods** (see **triangulation**).

Before thinking about qualitative research, researchers have to ask themselves about their hypotheses and the aim of the research itself. Is the purpose to explain or to understand the topic at hand? Is it a combination of the two? Apart from the obvious distinction between words and numbers, qualitative and quantitative methods have different requirements, strengths and weaknesses. These are what *ought* to affect researchers' decisions about which methodologies to use, so that they choose those best suited to their projects. The research questions of qualitative researchers may be similar to those of quantitative researchers (for example, 'Why do people abstain from voting?', 'Why do some revolutions succeed and others fail?'), but the emphasis is on detailed explanations that cannot be understood as existing outside of the explanations and justifications of those being studied.

The generally accepted view of qualitative research is that it is grounded in an interpretative (and natural) approach, attempting to understand why people view actions, values, beliefs and decisions, for example, as they do. How is it that we make sense of the world around us, yet different cultures and communities interpret that world differently? As Devine (2002: 197–8) states, 'It involves the researcher immersing himself or herself in the social setting in which they are interested, observing people in their usual milieu and participating in their activities.' This makes it very different from quantitative research, in which researchers need not have any contact or rapport with the subject being studied – in fact, in the case of large-*n* studies, where many thousands have responded to a survey, this would be virtually impossible. In qualitative methods, there is less emphasis on the need to study as many cases as possible. Also, while qualitative researchers will at times ask questions about representativeness and typicality, such requirements are not as central to claims regarding **reliability** and **validity** as they are in quantitative research, but, as Devine (2002: 205) states, they are no less important in terms of justifying research claims. Also, qualitative research is associated with an interpretive, rather than a positivist **epistemology**.

In order to address these types of questions, researchers can employ a number of tools, including **interviewing, focus groups** and **observation**, to name but three. For example, interviews allow researchers to capture the perspectives of the participants in their own words. The use of interviews as a method of data collection starts from the assumption that these people's views are knowledgeable, important, have meaning and can be made explicit. Most important is the assumption that these perspectives have (or will) *impact* the success of the research. By choosing to undertake interviews, researchers suggest that interpersonal contact is an important element in their research projects.

Other qualitative methods, which can be useful for evaluating research, include **documentary analysis** and **case studies**. Existing documents and records can often provide insight into an event, a particular time or group that cannot be observed by other means. These records come in various forms. Documents can be divided into two basic categories: public records and personal documents. Public records are created and archived for the purpose of providing an account and can usually be gathered with the research project in mind. Examples are official records such as *Hansard*, annual reports and newspaper archives. These all provide a useful sketch of general trends and patterns and are helpful in allowing for a better understanding of the project, participants and perhaps making comparisons between projects.

Other forms of public records are more focused on a particular group or topic, such as a research project on a non-governmental organisation. In such cases, researchers may want to gain access to *internal records*, such as minutes from meetings, policy reports, staff manuals or internal performance records. Such records could be vital to gaining an understanding of the institution's character and background and usually help the research in terms of envisaging strengths and weaknesses. Some organizations and groups are very protective of such data, but, if researchers do gain access to these documents, they can provide invaluable insights into the organisation's processes, priorities, concerns, values and resources.

The second category of documents is personal records and other first-hand knowledge of the topic being explored, be it an event or experience of a particular time and place. Such sources include diaries, personal correspondence, manuscripts, scrapbooks and even photographs. Individuals' personal documents can help researchers understand how one particular person sees (or saw) the world and how he or she interprets these visions.

The usefulness of documents as **primary sources** varies depending on whether or not they are easily obtained and, most importantly, if they are accurate. Documentary resources, more times than not, are useful in providing information about an organization's culture or the participants involved in a particular event and, in turn, this leads researchers to develop a set of evaluation or interview questions. Some of the disadvantages are that documents can be incomplete, access may be limited or difficult, time-consuming and there can be questions as to their authenticity or accuracy.

Bennett and Elman (2007: 111) have noticed a 'renaissance' in the use of qualitative methods in Political Science, now entering a third generation, and this is characterized by 'a new departure in terms of its methodological self-consciousness and rigor'. They identify the first generation of qualitative methods as extending to the early 1970s, covering interpretive, narrative and comparative approaches, while the second generation included 'classic' writings. Bennett and Elman (2007: 113) note:

> relatively little new work on qualitative methods seems to have affected the ways that political scientists carried out their research. This stands in sharp contrast to the many innovations that took place in statistical methods and formal modelling in this period.

Silverman (1993: 170) states that qualitative methods are 'especially interested in how ordinary people observe and describe their lives'. This means that such methods are useful for longitudinal research, which seeks to consider the individual dynamics of change. For example, the Negotiating Transitions to Citizenship project (Smith, 2003) was a three-year study of young people and citizenship. The aim of the project was to investigate young people's understandings and experiences of citizenship, including their sense of citizenship identity, and consider how and why these changed over time. While the project enabled the researchers to acquire a great volume of data, this in itself created additional methodological challenges as it was important that the study developed a structure and focus and the researchers had to decide how to analyse change.

FURTHER READING

Bennett, A. and Elman, C. (2007) 'Qualitative methods: The view from the subfields', *Comparative Political Studies*, 40 (2): 111–21.

Devine, F. (2002) 'Qualitative methods', in D. Marsh and G. Stoker (eds), *Theory and Methods in Political Science* (2nd edn). Houndmills, Basingstoke: Palgrave Macmillan.

King, G., Keohane, R.O. and Verba, S. (1994) *Designing Social Inquiry: Scientific inference in qualitative research*. Princeton, NJ: Princeton University Press.

Patton, M.Q. (1990) *Qualitative Evaluation and Research Methods* (2nd edn). London: Sage.

Ritchie, J. and Lewis, J. (eds) (2003) *Qualitative Research Practice: A guide for social science students and researchers*. London: Sage.

Seale, C. (2004) *Researching Society and Culture*. London: Sage.

Silverman, D. (1993) *Interpreting Qualitative Data*. London: Sage.

Vromen, A. (2010) 'Debating methods: Rediscovering qualitative methods', in D. Marsh and G. Stoker (eds), *Theory and Methods in Political Science* (3rd edn). Houndmills, Basingstoke: Palgrave Macmillan.

EXAMPLES

Bartolini, S. (1993) 'On time and comparative research', *Journal of Theoretical Politics*, 5 (2): 131–67.

Burman, E. (1997) 'Minding the gap: Positivism, psychology, and the politics of qualitative methods', *Journal of Social Issues*, 53 (4): 785–801.

Glasinka, A. (2006) 'Border ethnography and post-communist discourses of nationality in Poland', *Discourse & Society*, 17 (5): 609–26.

Katz, R. and Mair, P. (1995) 'Changing models of party organization and party democracy', *Party Politics*, 1(1): 5–28.

Kirchheimer, O. (1966) 'The transformation of the Western European party systems', in M. Weiner and J. LaPalombara (eds) *Political Parties and Political Development*. Princeton, N.J.: Princeton University Press.

Kitschelt, H. (1994) *The Transformation of European Social Democracy*. Cambridge: Cambridge University Press.

Rapley, T.J. (2001) 'The art(fullness) of open-ended interviewing: Some considerations on analysing interviews', *Qualitative Research*, 1 (3): 303–23.

Rokkan, S. (1970) *Citizens, Elections, Parties. Approaches to the Comparative Study of the Processes of Development*. Oslo: Universitetsforlaget.

Roulston, K. (2006) 'Close encounters of the "CA" kind: A review of literature analysing talk in research interviews', *Qualitative Research*, 6 (4): 515–34.

qualitative methods

Smith, N. (2003) 'Cross-sectional profiling and longitudinal analysis: Research notes on analysis in the longitudinal qualitative study, "Negotiating Transitions to Citizenship"', *International Journal of Social Research Methodology*, 6 (3): 273–7.

Quantitative Methods

We generally associate quantitative methods with the collection and analysis of large sets of data and the processes by which political information is transformed into quantifiable **variables**, enabling analysis via a range of statistical techniques. Although specific methods are not exclusive to particular epistemological approaches, it is nevertheless common to see particular subdisciplines of political analysis favouring quantitative or **qualitative methods** – **rational choice** being a good example of an approach prioritizing quantitative methods.

Quantitative methods are strongly associated with **positivism**. Researchers interested in the process and presentation of quantitative analysis can look to the many examples of articles published in journals such as *The British Journal of Political Science* and *The American Political Science Review*.

How do numerical data relate to what occurs in the world of politics and international relations? First, data may help us to understand how *often* something occurs. For example, we can measure the frequency of elections in each country or the amount of foreign aid awarded by international organizations. Second, we can compare and contrast *trends*. For example, do the countries donating foreign aid hold elections more frequently than the countries that are the recipients of that aid? We may also be able to make claims about relativity, saying, perhaps there is a correlation in recipient countries between the amount of foreign aid received over a ten-year period and the frequency of elections.

Grix (2002) refers to what he terms the 'Putnam School' as a label for an approach to explaining social capital. What links the researchers in this school, along with others with similar ontological and epistemological

key research concepts in
politics & international relations

views, is a methodological approach that prioritizes a quantitative strategy utilizing survey research. Grix gave it this name as, in his seminal text *Bowling Alone*, Putnam (2000) draws on a range of quantitative data (such as participation in politics and public affairs, group membership trends and patterns of trust and altruism) to make claims regarding the health of social capital in the USA.

By adopting quantitative methods, these researchers have been able to look for trends in relationships between variables in order to provide explanations and, occasionally, laws. For example, Downs' (1957) work on electoral competition and party system models sparked a wide-scale debate among political scientists such as Kirchheimer and Rokkan in the 1960s, Kitschelt from the late 1980s and Katz and Mair in the 1990s.

It is useful for researchers if independent variables change over time as they can measure the impact that this has on dependent variables. For example, if education levels increase, does this lead to higher levels of participation? If a country receives an increase in foreign aid, is this matched by a reduction in civil violence? We suggest that you also read the section on **variables** to appreciate some of the challenges that these researchers may face here.

The number of cases that are analysed is a central concern of quantitative research. It would, for example, be difficult to make claims about a population of 5 million if we had only studied 10 cases, but would we be confident if we had studied 1000 cases (see the section on **sampling**)?

The **presentation of quantitative analysis** is also an important consideration – long lists of numbers do little to assist an understanding of what is happening in terms of trends. The statistics can be presented in descriptive form – as frequencies, proportions and percentages in the form of tables, bar and pie charts – and the relationships between variables via bivariate or multivariate analysis (the former refers to the relationship between two variables, the latter to the relationships between many variables).

Despite the earlier observation that quantitative methods tend to be prioritized by particular **paradigms**, there have been shifts in more recent years that have attempted to weaken the quantitative versus qualitative divide. This can be seen in two ways. First, those researching themes 'typically' associated with qualitative research are engaging with quantitative methods. An interesting example of this is Weldon's (2004) study on feminist civil society. Weldon employs quantitative data for the:

- membership of national women's organizations
- number of feminist organizations
- number of women's centres
- number of rape crisis centres
- number of women's bookstores
- number of women's cultural festivals
- existence of a women's agenda project
- existence of a women's caucus in the legislature

to conduct an ordinary least squares (OLS) regression analysis in order to test whether women's self-organising facilitates empowerment to influence the pubic sphere of the United States.

Second, concepts of relevance to political and international relations researchers are deemed to have both quantitative *and* qualitative dimensions. This is highlighted by Thomas in her study of the convergence of the global development and security agendas. Thomas (2001: 162) draws attention to the fact that human security can be judged in terms of quantitative indicators (such as material sufficiency) and qualitative indicators (such as the achievement of human dignity, which incorporates personal autonomy, control over one's life and unhindered participation in the life of the community). While the two may correlate, it is possible to have relative financial wealth, but weak levels of qualitative security.

FURTHER READING

Grix, J. (2002) 'Introducing students to the generic terminology of social research', *Politics*, 22 (3): 175–86.

John, P. (2002) 'Quantitative methods', in D. Marsh and G. Stoker (eds), *Theory and Methods in Political Science* (2nd edn). Houndmills, Basingstoke: Palgrave Macmillan.

EXAMPLES

Downs, A. (1957) *An Economic Theory of Democracy*. New York: Harper Collins.

Putnam, R.D. (2000) *Bowling Alone: The collapse and revival of American community*. New York: Simon & Schuster.

Thomas, C. (2001) 'Global governance, development and human security: Exploring the links', *Third World Quarterly*, 22 (2): 159–75.

Weldon, S.L. (2004) 'The dimensions and policy impact of feminist civil society', *International Feminist Journal of Politics*, 6 (1): 1–28.

key research concepts in politics & international relations

Rational Choice

It is important to include the rational choice approach here as, unlike many political theories, it lends itself to particular methodological concerns and tools. As with some of the other methodological approaches deemed important for understanding political research methods, we can see interdisciplinary links – in this case with economics. This overlap is epitomized by Downs' (1957) classic text on competition between parties, while other arenas of politics addressed by rational choice include coalition theory (Riker, 1962), collective action (Olsen, 1971) and bureaucracy (Niskanen, 1971).

'Rational choice' is a generic term for a number of more specific models and explanations, such as public choice theory and game theory. It emerged as a part of the rise in **behaviouralism** (Ward, 2002: 65). Game theory in particular lends itself to debates within rational choice relating to arms races and nuclear deterrence.

Stoker (2006) argues that public choice theory offers an explanatory framework for political cynicism. Citing the work of Buchanan, he defines public choice as 'the science of political failure' (2006: 122), by which politicians and their influencing forces attempt to account for good governance via public choice theory (or, if we take the flipside of the coin, the failures of the state). Indeed, rational choice is often championed by theorists on the New Right (Ward, 2002: 70).

Dominant features of rational choice theory are the principles that:

- it is 'attempting to formulate a "science of politics" grounded on the discovery of empirical laws' (Hindmoor, 2006: 201), as with behaviouralism
- individuals make rational decisions that are underpinned by self-interest
- individual actions and beliefs can be explained via economic modelling, hence public choice theory tends to favour **quantitative methods**
- politicians and organizations behave like merchants who seek to sell their wares – citizens and voters are 'consumers' who purchase ideas and policies

- it is a deductive approach that attempts to demonstrate a logically coherent relationship between independent and dependent **variables**.

Criticism of public choice theory tends to focus on the apparent simplicity of the model – what exactly is rational? Is it a constant quality or far more contextual? How do we explain what appear to be more altruistic political decisions? For example, some political activists spend valuable time and other resources campaigning on issues that make little difference to their everyday physical circumstances. This has led to the development of the concept of bounded rationality (associated with the work of Simon, among others), which reflects the fact that individuals are not perfectly rational, but make what appear to be the most appropriate decisions based on limited information and demands of time.

FURTHER READING

Allingham, M. (2002) *Choice Theory: A very short introduction*. Oxford: Oxford University Press.

Elster, J. (ed.) (1987) *Rational Choice*. Oxford: Blackwell.

Hindmoor, A. (2006) *Rational Choice*. Houndmills, Basingstoke: Palgrave Macmillan.

Hindmoor, A. (2010) 'Rational choice', in D. Marsh and G. Stoker (eds), *Theory and Methods in Political Science* (3rd edn). Houndmills: Palgrave Macmillan.

Niskanen, W.A. (1971) *Bureaucracy and Representative Government*. Chicago, IL: Aldine-Atherton.

Olsen, M. (1971) *The Logic of Collective Action: Public goods and the theory of groups* (2nd edn). Cambridge, MA: Harvard University Press.

Riker, W.H. (1962) *The Theory of Political Coalitions*. New Haven, CT: Yale University Press.

Ward, H. (2002) 'Rational choice', in D. Marsh and G. Stoker (eds), *Theory and Methods in Political Science* (2nd edn). Houndmills, Basingstoke: Palgrave Macmillan.

EXAMPLES

Abrams, S., Iversen, T. and Soskice, D. (2010) 'Informal social networks and rational voting', *British Journal of Political Science*, 41 (2): 229–57.

Downs, A. (1957) *An Economic Theory of Democracy*. London: HarperCollins.

Hagermann, S. and Høyland, B. (2010) 'Bicameral politics in the European Union', *Journal of Common Market Studies*, 48 (4): 811–33.

key research concepts in politics & international relations

Hampsher-Monk, I. and Hindmoor, A. (2010) 'Rational choice and interpretive evidence: Caught between a rock and a hard place?', *Political Studies*, 58 (1): 47–65.

Howes, D.E. (2012) 'Torture is not a game: On the limitations and dangers of rational choice methods', *Political Research Quarterly*, 65 (1): 20–7.

Simon, H.A. (1957) *Models of Man*. New York: Wiley and Sons.

Stoker, G. (2006) *Why Politics Matters: Making democracy work*. Houndmills, Basingstoke: Palgrave Macmillan.

Realism

Realism is one of the main **paradigms** within International Relations. Indeed, arguably it constitutes the hegemonic paradigm as all other paradigms tend to be compared to realism.

Realist approaches seek to explain the behaviour of states, particularly in terms of military and strategic concerns. Realism is often called the *real* theory of political action. This comes from the view that it is derived from the German *Realpolitik* – a combination of the two words *real*, meaning substantive, and *politik*, meaning policy or politics. Whatever is the case realism is 'a many-mansioned tradition of thought' (Spegele, 1987: 189), starting with classical realism and onwards through to neo- or structural realism and neoclassical realism. These different currents, however, share common assumptions, not least of which is the claim that realism offers the 'true' picture when it comes to understanding and explaining international politics.

Classical realists, such as Morgenthau (1948), Kennan (1951) and Carr (2001), contend that the anarchical nature of the international system means strong states are allowed to do as they choose while relatively weaker states must do as they must. States are depicted as unitary, rational and atomistic actors within a Hobbesian environment. In this atmosphere of mutual suspicion and malign intent, states help themselves to security as there is no higher authority to defend them or, indeed, regulate their behaviour. Realists, then, see conflict as endemic

realism

125

to international relations rather than something that can be eradicated from it. Conflict can, at best, be managed via mechanisms such as the balance of power.

Classical realists believe that politics, like society in general, is governed by objective 'iron' laws that have their roots in human nature. Later realists, neorealists, follow the majority of the earlier assumptions, but, instead of focusing on human nature, they focus on the anarchical, relatively unchanging nature of the international system as the core driver of the behaviour of the state. Realism, focusing on the neutrality of the laws of politics, states that the operation of these laws is resistant to our preferences (both personal and/or national). It believes also, then, in the possibility of distinguishing in politics between truth and opinion – between what is true *objectively* and *rationally*, supported by evidence and illuminated by reason – and what is only a *subjective* judgement. Thus, from the position of the realist paradigm, a theory of politics must be subjected to the dual tests of reason and experience. The theory consists of seeking out 'facts' and giving them meaning via reason. For example, realism assumes that the character of a foreign policy can be established only by examining the political acts performed and the foreseeable consequences of these acts. Through these methods, according to the realist paradigm, we can find out what political leaders have actually done and, from the foreseeable consequences of their acts, we can work out what their objectives might have been.

For realists, the key to understanding international politics is the concept of political interest defined in terms of *power*. This concept provides the link between reason trying to understand international politics and the facts to be understood. By focusing on the concept of power, realism sets politics as an autonomous subject of action and understanding apart from other subjects, such as economics (understood in terms of political interest defined as wealth), **ethics** or even religion. Without such a concept of power (again national or personal) a **theory** of politics, international or domestic, would be altogether impossible, for without it we could not distinguish between political and non-political facts, nor could we bring order to the political world.

Take as an example that we assume our politicians think and act in terms of interest, defined as political power, and the evidence of past decisions bearing this out. That assumption allows us to track past actions and anticipate future ones, as it were – the steps a state takes to secure support for legislation, war and laws, past, present or future; in other words, the steps that *have been* taken or *will be* taken. Morgenthau (1978: 4–5) put it this way:

> We look over his [the politician's] shoulder when he writes his dispatches; we listen in on his conversation with other statesmen; we read and anticipate his very thoughts. Thinking in terms of interest defined as power, we think as he does, and as disinterested observers we understand his thoughts and actions perhaps better than he, the actor on the political scene, does himself.

By defining the concept of interest as political power we can, according to realism, understand the theory of politics without tainting what we observe with our own personal preferences (or subjectivity). Realism argues that, regardless of the individual politician's motivation, preferences or moral qualities, if state interest is defined in terms of power, policy generally will be consistent throughout time.

Neorealists moved further with the analysis of power, becoming more positivist than their predecessors. This is underscored by Waltz's deductive theoretical position and his focus on the relative distribution of capabilities between the states in the international system and the functional differentiation between states.

Post-neorealists, whether offensive realists (such as Mearsheimer) or defensive realists (such as Walt), also focus on states and power. The former adopt a 'more is never enough' approach, with the always insecure states ever ready to maximize their relative power over one another. The latter reject this view, claiming that states are more loss minimizers than power maximizers, wanting to maintain a sufficiency of power rather than a surfeit of it.

Neoclassical realists, such as Wohlforth, marry the systemic level of neorealism with the unit-level analysis of classical realism, fusing systemic **variables** such as the distribution of power between the units, including cognitive properties of the units, with variables from the realm of the domestic sphere, looking at the role of key policymakers, especially those within the 'national security or foreign policy executive' (Kitchen, 2010: 133). In terms of research methods, realists, especially neorealists, have tended to adopt means that can measure and assess what we can observe and have been critical of more interpretivist approaches (see **ontology**).

realism

127

A cautionary note: many students of Politics and International Relations make the mistaken assumption that the realist paradigm allows for no moral considerations. However, though it may seem impossible for politicians to act in such a morally neutral way, realism does not require (or really accept) indifference to political ideals and moral principles, but what it does require is a definitive distinction between what is politically desirable and the possible – between what is *desirable* everywhere and always and what is *possible* under the concrete circumstances of the particular time and place in which a decision is made.

FURTHER READING

Carr, E.H. (2001) *The Twenty Years' Crisis, 1919–1939: An introduction to the study of international relations* (2nd edn). Houndmills, Basingstoke: Palgrave Macmillan.

Kennan, G. (1951) *American Diplomacy, 1900–1950*. New York: New American Library.

Kitchen, N. (2010) 'Systemic pressures and domestic ideas: A neoclassical realist model of grand strategy formation', *Review of International Studies*, 36 (1): 117–44.

Mearsheimer, J.J. (2001) *The Tragedy of Great Power Politics*. New York: W.W. Norton.

Morgenthau, H.J. (1948) *Politics Among Nations: The struggle for power and peace*. New York: Alfred A. Knopf.

Morgenthau, H.J. (1978) *Politics Among Nations: The struggle for power and peace* (5th edn). London: Alfred A. Knopf.

Walt, S. (1985) 'Alliance formation and the balance of world power', *International Security*, 9 (4): 3–43.

Walt, S. (2002) 'The enduring relevance of the realist tradition', in I. Katznelson and H.V. Milner (eds), *Political Science: State of the discipline*. New York: W.W. Norton.

Waltz, K.N. (1979) *Theory of International Politics*. Reading, MA: Addison-Wesley.

Wohlforth, W.C. (1993) *The Elusive Balance: Power and perceptions during the Cold War*. Ithaca, NY: Cornell University Press.

EXAMPLES

Kirshner, J. (2012) 'The tragedy of offensive realism: Classical realism and the rise of China', *European Journal of International Relations*, 18 (1): 53–75.

Rosato, S. and Schuessler, J. (2011) 'A realist foreign policy for the United States', *Perspectives on Politics*, 9 (4): 803–19.

Rynning, S. (2011) 'Realism and the common security and defence policy', *Journal of Common Market Studies*, 49 (1): 23–42.

Schmidt, B.C. (2008) 'The Bush doctrine and the Iraq War: Neoconservatives versus realists', *Security Studies*, 17 (2): 191–220.

Spegele, R. (1987) 'Three forms of political realism', *Political Studies*, 35 (2): 189–210.

Reliability

When discussing **validity**, we stress the importance of theoretical relevance to **empirical analysis**. Similarly, when establishing reliability, we seek to identify consistency in our research findings. Reliability is important as it is one of the elements required to establish the validity of research.

To understand reliability, think in terms of a non-political example. In order to attend classes regularly, you probably rely on your alarm on your mobile phone to wake you up in the morning. The reliability of your alarm depends on several factors – you have charged your phone and have remembered to set the alarm – and if any one of these is not in place, it is possible you will miss your class.

Within political research, we can ensure reliability by applying consistent **methods**. In relation to voting behaviour, for example, in order to track patterns of change in voters' choices, we need to ensure that our **methodology** is consistent, which we can achieve in several ways. First, we need to make sure we ask the same questions – if we change the wording, even the order of the questions, we cannot expect to get the same responses. Second, we need to ensure that we are studying the same research population. If we are interested in first-time voters, there is little point in asking pensioners – many will have taken the opportunity to vote before.

Manheim and Rich (1991) identify three general methods of assessing the reliability of measures within social sciences, which are the:

- test–retest method
- alternative form method
- subsample method.

Reliability is most commonly ascertained by retesting research questions to establish the consistency of the data collected. We can see that this happens frequently in opinion polling, for example, where the public are often asked to evaluate political leadership qualities and policy decisions or register party support. However, just because we attempt to ensure reliability by being consistent in our methodological approach does not mean we can always eliminate unreliable responses that may occur due to problems of memory or desirability. Imagine you are carrying out a longitudinal survey. You ask the same people the same questions on a regular basis and find that some respondents are actually becoming younger, not older. Attractive as this may seem, it is not reliable (and may lead us to question the reliability of their other responses). Memory can also impact what people *think* they have done, rather than what they *actually* did. For example, Fisher (2007: 600) identifies a problem for survey-based studies of electoral behaviour, where there is a tendency for turnouts to be over-reported:

> While the best quality national election studies often find differences just outside the range of sampling error between the official results and the distribution of the vote amongst the survey respondents, there is a much more substantial and systematic problem with measures of turnout … about half of this is due to false reporting by respondents, as validation exercises with official records in Britain and the United States have shown.

The 'problem', therefore, is not respondents deliberately misleading the researcher, but a simple problem of recollection.

However, we must also accept that responses may genuinely change over time. The world of politics and international relations would be rather dull if opinions and attitudes remained completely stable. In the real world of research, relatively few studies can afford the luxury of being longitudinal, in which participants can be requestioned. Similarly, the qualities of the research population that interest us may make requestioning impossible – a voter can only be a first-time voter once.

An alternative method of ascertaining reliability is intercoding, or interobserver reliability. This occurs when we ask several researchers to 'judge' a coding system. If researchers concur on coding, then we can have more trust in the claim that reliability is ensured. This may be particularly important, for example, when coding specific occupations into similar groups. We can see an example of intercoding in Marsh and Savigny's (2004) analysis of Political Science. The intention here was to question claims made by other researchers about the discipline of Political Science. Marsh and Savigny's concern was that a dominant 'American' view was being articulated (and this is a particularly positivist view). Each author coded the relevant content of journal articles independently and agreed in almost every case, enabling them to claim that 'results are robust' (2004: 161).

Therefore, as researchers, we need to pay close attention to methodological reliability in order to ensure as high a level of data reliability as possible. This is a challenge identified by Sanders et al. (2002) in relation to British Election Study surveys. They (2002: 194) demonstrate that the process by which questions are asked may impact responses regarding which party voters identify with – this being 'the stable and enduring attachment that a voter feels towards a particular political party' – and cite a range of independent studies that indicate the British Election Study historically overestimated partisanship. If you are relying on secondary data for your analysis, it is important therefore to give careful consideration to what exactly that data is measuring and the extent to which it is 'fit-for-purpose' for your own research.

The emphasis on 'retesting' to ensure reliability becomes a much more problematic challenge when applied to qualitative analysis. Issues such as representativeness are dealt with differently and the breadth and quantity of data are less important than its depth. As a result, reliability is judged in a different manner. Armstrong et al. (1997) explain the challenge this caused for their own study of **focus groups'** perceptions of disability and genetic screening. This involved six researchers taking part in inter-rater reliability, with some degree of agreement: 'the six analysts did identify similar themes but there were significant differences in the way they were "packaged"' (Armstrong et al., 1997: 599). While the categories were subject to little disagreement, the label applied to such categories was not so easily agreed on, thus raising important questions about 'the level at which concordance might be expected' (Armstrong et al., 1997: 601).

FURTHER READING

Manheim, J.B. and Rich, R.C. (1991) *Empirical Political Analysis* (3rd edn), London: Longman. pp. 67–9.

Pennings, P., Keman, H. and Kleinnijenhuis, J. (1999) *Doing Research in Political Science*. London: Sage. pp. 85–90.

EXAMPLES

Armstrong, D., Gosling, A., Weinman, J. and Marteau, T. (1997) 'The place of inter-rater reliability in qualitative research: An empirical study', *Sociology*, 31 (3): 597–606.

Fisher, S.D. (2007) '(Change in) turnout and (change in) the left share of the vote', *Electoral Studies*. 26 (3): 598–611.

Marsh, D. and Savigny, H. (2004) 'Political sciences as a broad church: The search for a pluralist discipline', *Politics*, 24 (3): 155–68.

Sanders, D., Burton, J. and Kneeshaw, J. (2002) 'Identifying the true party indentifiers: A question wording experiment', *Party Politics*, 8 (2): 193–205.

reliability

The world of politics and international relations is vast, made up of many countries, organizations and societies, and it is often the case that it is physically impossible to research every individual member (in terms of time, cost and access). Therefore, much political research relies on the sampling of research populations – we study some cases in order to make generalizations about the group as a whole. In relation to measuring public opinion, sampling theory tells us that a carefully selected sample of 1000 people will give a very good indication of the views of the population. As Fielding and Gilbert (2000: 226) state, 'It is quite rare for it to be sensible to conduct a census, that is, to obtain data from everyone in the population. By measuring just those in a sample, time and money can be saved that are better used on other aspects of the research, while still obtaining sufficient accuracy for valid conclusions to be drawn.'

The first stage in applying sampling is to identify the research population – that is, the collective group of people who share a common characteristic. This may be those who are registered to vote, those who are elected representatives or those who are members of certain campaigning organizations. Those who are members of the research population provide the sampling frame (Burnham et al., 2004: 86):

> The sampling frame is the list of units from which the sample is to be drawn. The choice of sampling frame will depend on what lists of the population are available and how accurate they are. The choice will also depend on the subject of the research.

Clearly, there is going to be a relationship between the accuracy of the sampling frame and the ability to choose a representative sample. Unsurprisingly, the first and often significant challenge that a researcher will need to overcome is locating population lists, particularly if the research population is large and likely to change on a frequent basis. For example, electoral registers are updated at regular points, but if you are researching an area with a very mobile population, this source will quickly become unreliable. A sampling error may occur if the proportion in the sample is different from its true value in the population as a whole.

key research concepts in politics & international relations

Depending on the sampling techniques used, we may or may not be able to make confident **inferences** about the research population (see **causality and correlations**). Being able to make inferences based on the relationship between independent **variables** and dependent variables can be a complicated process. There is no 'set figure' for how large or small a sample should be and, as Payne and Payne (2004: 201) state, it is likely to be determined by three factors:

- the resources available, including financial and access issues
- planned analysis method
- the homogeneity or heterogeneity of the research population.

> In the end the sample size must take into account the degree of diversity in the population on key variables, the level of sampling error that is tolerable and the reliability required of the sample. Decisions about one factor have implications for other factors. (de Vaus, 2004: 81)

Once we progress beyond research populations that are relatively small in size and easy to identify, our opportunities for probabilistic sampling are reduced. A common misunderstanding among students untrained in appropriate research methods is that standing in the middle of a town centre and asking passers by to respond to a questionnaire is the equivalent of probabilistic, or random, sampling. It is not, as you will find very different people in the centre of town depending on the day of the week and even the time of day. The 'typical person in the street' will vary, for example, by age and occupation depending on whether you are carrying out your survey at 9 a.m. or 9 p.m.

Probabilistic sampling can take the following forms:

- A random sample, in which every member of the research population has an equal chance of being selected. de Vaus (2004: 71) stipulates that random sampling is, to a large extent, reliant on the existence of a good sampling frame. A key advantage of random sampling is that 'it is free of the systematic bias that might stem from choices made by the researcher' (Gorard, 2003: 67). However, many research studies you may come across will include 'case studies' of particular social or geographic groups, the justification being that certain groups are easier to access in practice than others.
- A systematic sample is a frequently used technique when the sampling frame takes the form of an address, telephone or e-mail

directory. The sample is created by selecting every *n*th case – for example, you could send a questionnaire to every tenth e-mail address in a long list. Yet, this can be problematic for, as de Vaus (2004: 73) claims, 'a certain *type* of person may recur at regular intervals within the sampling frame. If the sampling fraction is such that it matches this interval, the sample will include only certain types of people and systematically exclude others.'

- A stratified sample entails dividing the sampling frame into sub-groups or strata and then taking random samples from each. This may be useful if we believe that particular relevant variables are under-represented in our research population and this scarcity does not lead to a lack of representation in the sample. We could, for example, stratify university students by age categories to ensure older students (such as those over 30) are not absent from the sample.

- A cluster sample is used if we wish to study a research population that is widely dispersed, particularly when we have limited resources for completing the data-collection process. As Gorard (2003: 70) notes, 'Using a clustered sample implies not so much a difference in selection procedures as a difference in defining population units. The cases we are interested in often occur in natural clusters such as institutions'. We might, for example, construct a study that is interested in black and ethnic minority (BME) political participation and the impact of critical mass – that is, are patterns of participation in areas of high BME density different from that in areas with low BME density? Electoral wards may form the source of our clusters (or what we would term cases), with potential participants then being selected by random or stratified sampling.

You may also see reference to 'booster samples', but this is not a sampling method per se, it is a strategy adopted by researchers to ensure the representation of a particular research population subgroup is large enough to make confident claims without having to substantially increase the sample size for the entire study. Booster samples have been applied to Scottish, Welsh and ethnic minority strands of the British Election Studies at various times.

There are often very practical reasons for adopting non-probabilistic sampling and this is often underpinned by an inability to locate a reliable sampling frame. Gorard (2003: 72) suggests that it is most appropriate to use non-probabilistic sampling in research design, particularly in pilot studies for trialling the research design rather than gathering data per se. Non-probabilistic sampling can take the following forms:

- A snowball sample, in which the researcher uses a small number of contacts to generate a larger sample group. For Devine (1992), this was a useful technique as her study of car workers took place during a period of poor industrial relations, but she found that speaking to a small group of respondents opened up the opportunity to expand her list of contacts. The challenge of such a sampling approach lies with the fact that 'the quality of the sample depends on the starting point, and strength, of the network' (Payne and Payne, 2004: 210). This was a problem encountered by Lupton and Tulloch (2002: 321) in their Australian study of notions of risk in society. Snowball sampling was used to recruit participants, but 'this strategy, however, was only partly successful in achieving a heterogeneous group of interviewees, as the group was dominated by well-educated, young and middle-aged adults of British ancestry.'
- A quota sample relies on the selection of characteristics to reflect their distribution within the research population. So, if we know that 10 per cent of university students are over 30, we select a sample that reflects this quota. However, the researchers may be selecting a sample that is not altogether typical – that is, while the required characteristics may be matched, the sample may be substantially different in other ways. As Payne and Payne (2004: 212) say, 'The danger is that interviewers select those easiest to contact, or who seem friendly and approachable, whose answers may not be representative.'
- A volunteer, or convenience, sample is commonly employed in 'popularity polls' – the kind commonly conducted by television and radio programmes in which audiences are invited to phone or text in their choice of winner or 'evictee'. Political researchers are unlikely to use this approach, however, and certainly would not attempt to make claims about representativeness, as those who choose to express their views often have a motive for doing so.

FURTHER READING

Burnham, P., Gilland Lutz, K., Grant, W. and Layton-Henry, Z. (2004) *Research Methods in Politics*. Houndmills, Basingstoke: Palgrave Macmillan.

de Vaus, D (2004) *Surveys in Social Research* (4th edn). Abingdon: Routledge.

Fielding, J. and Gilbert, N. (2000) *Understanding Social Statistics*. London: Sage.

Gorard, S. (2003) *Quantitative Methods in Social Science*. London: Continuum.

Payne, G. and Payne, J. (2004) *Key Concepts in Research Methods*. London: Sage.

Sanders, D., Clarke, H.D., Stewart, M.C., Whiteley, P.F. and Twyman, J. (2004) 'The 2001 British election study internet poll: a methodological experiment', *Journal of Political Marketing*, 3 (4): 29–55.

sampling

EXAMPLES

Devine, F. (1992) *Affluent Workers Revisited: Privatism and the working class.* Edinburgh: Edinburgh University Press.

Lupton, D. and Tulloch, J. (2002) '"Risk is part of your life": Risk epistemologies among a group of Australians', *Sociology*, 36 (2): 317–34.

Whiteley, P.F. and Seyd, P. (1988) 'The dynamics of party activism in Britain: A spiral of demobilization?', *British Journal of Political Science*, 28 (1): 113–37.

Secondary Analysis

As a researcher, you may be engaged in the process of creating new data, be it by carrying out a survey, **interviewing** political actors or analysing the content of news stories, and this is referred to as primary data analysis. However, it is often the case that we re-evaluate existing quantitative and qualitative data. This may be because we do not have the time or resources to create new data or we may not be able to access those we wish to study (imagine you want to contrast attitudes towards human rights over a long period). Indeed, much comparative analysis is based on the existence of secondary data sources in multiple countries. For example, Inglehart and Norris' (2003) study of gender equality made extensive use of two existing surveys – the World Values Survey and the European Values Survey. These studies cover more than 70 societies, which themselves account for over 80 per cent of the world's population. There are strong arguments for utilizing existing data to carry out new analyses, particularly when this data has been located in public archives (see, for example, www.esrc.ac.uk and www.data-archive.ac.uk).

Secondary analysis involves more than merely quoting an existing study – it implies the reanalysis of data. In reanalysing existing data, there are several concerns we have to take into account. First, we do not have the same level of control over existing data as when creating our own. A subtle change in the wording of questions (see **reliability** and **survey design**) can produce different responses, so it is important to be

key research concepts in politics & international relations

absolutely clear about the environment in which data was generated and how relevant it is to our own research question. One technique we can utilize is that of creating derived **variables** – that is, creating a new variable from the responses to several others (Arber and Ginn, cited in Slater, 1988: 200).

Second, we can ask different questions depending on whether the data is in raw or aggregate format (see **levels of measurement**). The advantage of aggregate data is that it is easy to manage, but it only allows us to understand general trends, we cannot make claims about specific individual cases. In addition, it may be that different studies have not coded variables in a consistent way. An oft-quoted example is the 'UK official' definition of unemployment, which was altered on over 20 occasions during the 1980s (see **official data**).

While secondary analysis of qualitative data may not face the same challenges of coding, there are ethical concerns – should such data be used for a purpose other than that for which it was originally intended? In addition, doing so undermines one of the strengths of **qualitative methods**, as noted by Devine (1995), which is the researcher's direct experience of the social and political setting.

The advantages and disadvantages of conducting a secondary analysis can by understood by considering opinion poll data. Political opinion polling began in the United States of America and large-scale surveys have become increasingly common. However, different companies use different polling processes, ask questions differently and present final predictions in a manner that means we often do not see the 'raw data' – only the aggregated, and sometimes 'weighted', results. Unless we have access to longitudinal studies, we must bear in mind the 'snapshot' element of opinion polling – we can only expect a poll to be reflective of that opinion among those people, at that time. Consistency and stability of opinion may exist, but we cannot assume that it does.

Differences in the wording of questions – however slight they may seem – can substantially affect the comparability of polling data. Single-response questions may not be sufficient as the meaning, or context, of responses can change over time. The problem here lies in the fact that the same terms can have different meanings over time and, 'asked over several decades … the meaning of responses to questions … becomes completely indeterminate' (Dunleavy, 1990: 457). So, we can end up classifying together people with quite dissimilar views because the wording has become decontextualized. The following is an example of the impact that this factor can have on research.

A study by Farrall (2004: 169) focused on exploring what people mean when they say that they are 'afraid of crime' and made the following criticism of the extent to which surveys can accurately tap into emotional responses to crime:

> to claim that we cannot alter question styles or wording because this will leave redundant earlier data is nothing short of an admission that question wording influences data, and that changes in question styles will result in changes in the data 'produced', ... and therefore that survey-research 'reality' is methodology dependent.

FURTHER READING

Devine, F. (1995) 'Qualitative analysis', in D. Marsh and G. Stoker (eds), *Theory and Methods in Political Science*. London: Macmillan.

Dunleavy, P. (1990) 'Mass political behaviour: Is there more to learn?', *Political Studies*, 38 (2): 453–69.

Slater, D. (1988) 'Using official statistics', in C. Seale (ed.), *Researching Society and Culture*. London: Sage. pp. 197–201.

EXAMPLES

Farrall, S. (2004) 'Revisiting crime surveys: Emotional responses without emotions? OR Look back at anger', *International Journal of Social Research Methodology*, 7 (2): 157–71.

Inglehart, R. and Norris, P. (2003) *Rising Tide: Gender equality and cultural change around the world*. Cambridge: Cambridge University Press.

Survey Design

Surveys are used in the measurement of behaviour, attitudes and opinions. They generally generate quantitative data (telling researchers 'what' but not 'why'). The term 'survey' refers to the data that is collected (often in the form of short answers that can then be transformed into a quantitative format in order to conduct statistical analyses). This is not to be confused with a 'questionnaire', which is the tool by means of which the survey data is collected. A questionnaire consists of a series of questions or statements on a form that respondents complete and it is *standardized* – that is, the same questions are asked, in the same order and the same wording is used.

Questionnaires utilize two types of question:

- open – a blank space is left for respondents to fill in their answer
- closed – a list of alternatives is provided for respondents to select the most appropriate answer.

A potential problem with closed questions is that the 'right answer' – in the sense that it is closest to the respondent's view rather than being correct or incorrect – may not be available. This creates the problem of false opinion (de Vaus, 1996). An advantage, though, is that surveys using them can generalize large amounts of data relatively quickly, allowing generalizations to be made about the wider population.

The use of questionnaires is strongly associated with the empirical research tradition as the thinking is that there is 'factual information' out there we can identify and measure. Survey data enables us to:

- explain social and political phenomena – for example, the General Lifestyle Survey (formerly the General Household Survey) asks a range of questions about family, lifestyle and income in order to monitor policy
- track trends – for example, the General Lifestyle Survey has identified a decline in average household size and a growth in the proportion of the population living alone, both of which have implications for what kinds of housing are needed, and increases in the proportion of families headed by a lone parent and the percentage of people cohabiting
- make predictions – for example, opinion poll data is frequently used to predict election outcomes, but perhaps more reliable is demographic information, which enables forecasters to see if populations are living longer and birthrates declining, for example, and, if both are the case, then governments may feel it is more useful to allocate resources to healthcare rather than education
- use an alternative to interviews – for example, if we are dealing with sensitive or contentious political issues, such as Blair's (1999) research on the attitudes of Conservative MPs towards the Maastricht Treaty.

There are important epistemological assumptions underpinning survey-based research. We need to focus on some very practical issues:

- Who do we want to study? Research populations and **sampling**.
- How are we going to gather the information? We can choose from verbal, self-completion, telephone and Internet questionnaires. It is interesting to note that American professional survey organizations prefer to employ middle-age women as interviewers because respondents do not find them intimidating (Manheim and Rich, 1995: 160).

How do we 'tap into' the precise information that we require for the research? Marsh (1979) suggests that there are questions we should routinely ask about any questionnaire. Some general concerns are the following:

- How important is the issue to the people interviewed? The extent to which an issue makes a difference to what someone thinks or does is referred to as *salience* (Broughton, 1995). For example, respondents will be more likely to have an opinion on the funding of public transport if they travel to work by a bus, train or tram than if they drive or cycle.
- How was the question worded? Research has shown that the wording of the questions can be influential. We should avoid:

  o presumptive questions (Leech, 2002)
  o overly complex questions – for accurate responses the questions need to be kept as straightforward as possible, which includes avoiding double negatives in a sentence
  o ambiguous questions – if we consider the statement 'violent criminals deserve to be deprived of some of their human rights', we can see that 'some' is a vague term and, as such, may generate vague answers
  o embarrassing and sensitive questions – clearly there are topics that people are comfortable to talk about with strangers and others they are not, so, in some questionnaires, sensitive questions appear at the end as interviewers may have built up some sort of rapport with the respondents by then, so they may then be less likely to refuse to answer them
  o double-barrelled questions – do not ask for more than one piece of information per question.

- Marsh (1979: 284) rather cynically observes, 'Polls are not socially scientific; they are not democratic; they are often employed so as to reconfirm their own results; but most importantly they may be used to confer a kind of legitimacy to those people who can quote their results ... It is this appearance of ultra-democracy that gives them their power'. So, as Dunleavy (1990: 457) states in his critique of survey-based research of mass political behaviour, 'how questions are phrased is of the first importance to the ways in which they can subsequently be analysed'. He is concerned that early British election studies have ignored context, such as the importance of neighbourhood, socialization processes and local politics, although studies carried out since the early 1990s have begun to address this omission. Similarly, Burnham et al. (2004: 95) note, 'It is often believed that question wording is the major source of errors in surveys because small changes in wording or even different emphases put on words by interviewers might lead to large differences in responses which would not otherwise exist.'
- Does the order in which questions appear matter? Research has shown that order can be influential (Leech, 2002). Indeed, Bernstein and Dyer (1992: 95) point out that 'some questions may influence the responses to other questions on the same questionnaire'. An additional criticism of survey research is that, rather than gaining honest responses, some questions can push respondents to respond in particular ways. Bartle (1999) suggests that the British Election Studies questionnaire might encourage respondents to give the same response to the questions on reported vote and party identification because the latter immediately follows the former. As a result, people who do not consider themselves as identifying with a party will report identifying with the party they currently prefer, 'thus inflating the strength of relationship between party identification and vote' (Bartle, 1999: 123).

The number of questions contained in a survey will depend on the nature of the research population. If it is an elite study, respondents may be willing to give it a fair amount of their time, but, if it is a general survey, it is important to keep the questionnaire as short as possible or some will be discouraged from participating. In this case, serious consideration needs to be given to the **variables** that the survey will incorporate.

By offering open questions, attention can be paid to how to code the answers (if a **quantitative analysis** is to be carried out) once the data has been collected. If closed questions are opted for, then it is necessary to consider coding requirements in advance. A pilot study not only helps to explore the impact of the order of the questions and their wording, but whether or not the questionnaire as a whole is appropriate for gaining an understanding of the target research population (de Vaus, 1996).

In order to judge whether or not an existing or designed questionnaire is 'good', researchers need to reflect on the intention behind including such a research strategy. The type of survey employed – and, thus, the questionnaire used to collect the survey data – will depend on who we want to question and what we want to know. The main types of survey are as follows:

- Mass surveys – if we are interested in the responses of the general population.
- Elite surveys – for when we are 'interviewing people who are defined by their position as being important in some way' (Bernstein and Dyer, 1992: 91). As such, they have particular knowledge that is central to the survey, possibly due to their occupation or membership of a political group.
- Cross-sectional surveys – for when we ask our respondents to complete the survey on one occasion only. Thus, they provide 'a snapshot of a moving target' (Manheim and Rich, 1995: 132). It is important to note that, particularly in relation to political opinions, the responses gained might be very different if we had conducted the survey at an earlier or later date, due to the potential influence of events and experience.
- Longitudinal surveys – for when we want to survey respondents on more than one occasion to look for stability or changes in attitudes and opinions. This may be achieved via *trend surveys*, in which different people are surveyed from the same population (a trend survey of members of a political party might want to find out why new members join the party). *Cohort*, or *panel, surveys* focus on the same sample of people over a period of time (for example, the British Election Panel Studies) in order to measure changes in opinions. A potential problem with longitudinal panel surveys (apart from the fact that they can make the research expensive) is the opportunity for *reactivity* – that is, 'the reaction of human subjects to the knowledge that they are being investigated' (Wilson, 1996: 95), who may actually become more interested and more knowledgeable about a topic because they know they are going to be surveyed again. In addition, panel surveys may be subject to attrition, which is when people drop out of the

study (they might become fed up with repeatedly being surveyed or move and become uncontactable), and this might affect the study's representativeness.

Does the delivery method affect response rates? Face-to-face surveys should have a response rate of between 60 and 85 per cent. Telephone surveys may have slightly lower response rates as respondents are more likely to terminate a survey by putting down the phone than they are to try to walk away in a face-to-face situation. Self-completion and mail questionnaires inevitably have lower response rates. For example, Wring et al.'s study of first-time voters had a response rate of 32 per cent, although Whiteley et al.'s (1994) postal survey of Conservative Party members had a much more impressive rate of 63 per cent. That does not imply the latter was a 'better' or more worthwhile survey, but maybe more indicative of the survey population and their propensity to respond to such a research request. The key 'challenge' is not that some people will not respond, but that non-respondents are not randomly distributed in the sample (Burnham et al., 2004: 99).

FURTHER READING

Bartle, J. (1999) 'Improving the measurement of party identification in Britain', in J. Fisher, P. Cowley, D. Denver and A. Russell (eds), *The British Elections and Parties Review: Volume 9*. London: Frank Cass.

Bernstein, R.A. and Dyer, J.A. (1992) *An Introduction to Political Science Methods* (3rd edn). Upper Saddle River, NJ: Prentice Hall.

Berrens, R.P., Bohara, A.K., Jenkins-Smith, H., Silva, C. and Weimer, D.L. (2003) 'The advent of Internet surveys for political research: A comparison of telephone and Internet samples', *Political Analysis*, 11 (1): 1–22.

Broughton, D. (1995) *Public Opinion Polling and Politics in Britain*. Hemel Hempstead: Harvester Wheatsheaf.

Burnham, P., Gilland Lutz, K., Grant, W. and Layton-Henry, Z. (2004) *Research Methods in Politics*. Houndmills, Basingstoke: Palgrave Macmillan.

de Vaus, D. (1996) *Surveys in Social Research* (4th edn). London: UCL Press.

Holbrook, A.L., Green, M.C. and Krosnick, J.A. (2003) 'Telephone versus face-to-face interviewing of national probability samples with long questionnaires: Comparisons of respondent satisficing and social desirability response bias', *Public Opinion Quarterly*, 67: 79–125.

Leech, B.L. (2002) 'Interview methods in political science', *PS: Political Science and Politics*, 35 (4): 663–64.

Manheim, J.B. and Rich, R.C. (1995) *Empirical Political Analysis* (4th edn). New York: Longman.

survey design

Marsh, C. (1979) 'Opinion polls: Social science or political manoeuvre?', in J. Irvine, I. Miles and J. Evens (eds), *Demystifying Social Statistics*. London: Pluto.

Wilson, M. (1996) 'Asking questions', in R. Sapsford and V. Jupp (eds), *Data Collection and Analysis*. London: Sage.

EXAMPLES

Blair, A. (1999) 'Question time: Questionnaires and Maastricht', *Politics*, 19 (2): 117–24.

Dunleavy, P. (1990) 'Mass political behaviour: Is there more to learn?', *Political Studies*, 38 (2): 453–69.

General Lifestyle Survey, formerly General Household Survey, available online at: www.esds.ac.uk/government/ghs (accessed 11 September 2012)

Whiteley, P., Seyd, P. and Richardson, J. (1994) *True Blues: The politics of Conservative Party membership*. Oxford: Oxford University Press.

Wring, D., Henn, M. and Weinstein, M. (1999) 'Young people and contemporary politics: Committed scepticism or engaged cynicism?', in J. Fisher, P. Cowley, D. Denver and A. Russell (eds), *The British Elections and Parties Review: Volume 9*. London: Frank Cass.

Theory

Theory is essential to political analysis and activism as it 'provides us with a means through which we can analyze, explain, understand and potentially change the world' (Savigny and Marsden, 2011: 5). Theory helps us to critically engage with political phenomena so that Political Science moves beyond description and storytelling. Our understanding of the empirical world, then, is enhanced by the theoretical underpinnings of our study. Theory facilitates this critical engagement in a number of ways. It allows us to interpret our data in a systematic and ordered way. Our theoretical approach lets us represent the complexity of the political world, with its plurality of actors and processes and plethora of institutions and issues, in a more manageable form. We can identify and categorize those phenomena that we find have the greatest importance and focus our enquiry on them. Theory helps us to answer the 'Why?'

questions in political study, moving us on from the 'What?', 'When?' and 'Where?' As Stoker (1995: 16–17) writes, theory:

> helps us to see the wood for the trees. Good theories select out certain factors as the most important or relevant if one is interested in providing an explanation of an event. Without such a sifting process no effective observation can take place. The observer would be buried under a pile of detail and be unable to weight the influence of different factors in explaining an event.

We can explain why certain events happen or fail to occur, why some situations prevail and whether or not they must do so. Critical theorists, such as neo-Gramscians, some constructivists and some feminists, especially, engage with this latter consideration as they explicitly use theory to challenge the dominant social world (Rengger and Thirkell-White, 2007: 6):

> The search for the possibilities of change should be anchored in an emancipatory project that seeks, not just the possibility of change as such, but rather points to change in a certain – progressive – direction.

A key critical theorist, the neo-Gramscian Robert Cox (1981: 128), observed that 'theory is always for someone, always for some purpose'. We need to appreciate, whether we subscribe to critical theories or not, that theory is never neutral. When we read a scholar's narrative of events or someone's interpretation of the political world, it is important to remember that these are subjective renditions. Theory is used to interpret data – the data themselves do not explain or analyse, but, rather, the researchers use the data in accordance with their particular theoretical approaches. These approaches determine which aspects of the data are privileged in the researcher's analysis. Different theories emphasize different **variables** in their contending accounts of political behaviour. Different theories have different underpinning ontological and epistemological assumptions concerning which unit/level of analysis has primacy in explaining politics and international relations. Realist theories, for example, are state-centric in their approach and so emphasize the role of the state in their analyses. Classical realists adopt a state level of analysis, treating the state as a unitary and egotistical actor. Structural realists, too, seek to explain why the state acts as it does and look at the impact of the international system as a determinant of state

theory

145

behaviour. In contrast, constructivist accounts tend to focus on a wide range of interconnected domestic and transnational actors, processes and institutions, with an emphasis on the importance of ideational factors in their analysis. Other levels of analysis, such as the individual, the sub-state and the transnational are utilized rather than simply that of the state. Instead of a focus on the State's quest for survival and power as the driver within international politics, attention is given to a wider cast of actors and a range of motivations, notably including those drawn from ideational phenomena.

Theories differ, then, not only in terms of which actors and factors they regard as most influential in explaining political behaviour but also which level(s) of analysis they find most useful. Realists tend to focus on the state level, the systemic level or an interplay of both levels of analysis. Marxist accounts tend to focus on the interconnection of systemic forces and modes of production and capitalism. In contrast, theories of foreign policy analysis, for example, stress the central role of human agency in decision-making and use the individual or the group level of analysis.

The 'level of analysis' chosen affects the questions to be posed by researchers and they use a level of analysis that accords with their ontological and epistemological positions. The levels of analysis help to differentiate between actors and processes as well as analyse their interactions – although we must remain vigilant to the danger of **ecological fallacy**.

Theory, then, is used to simplify the world around us, order it and make it manageable in order to enable a coherent analysis. Some theories tend to simplify complexity more than others, as they are more parsimonious than others. Such parsimony superficially may be very attractive to students. Ultimately, however, the more parsimonious the theory, the more reductionist might be its scope and the less persuasive its explanations. Neorealism, for example, as found in the work of Waltz (1990), is frequently criticized for its narrowness of focus on 'the logic of anarchy' at the systemic level of analysis, which then impacts state behaviour.

Theories tend to be amalgams of normative and empirical concerns. Essentially, normative political theory comprises theorizing about 'what ought to be' rather than 'what is' and it has a rich tradition within political research. The works of Aristotle, for example, and the quest for a 'good society' may be seen as the core rationale of Politics as a discipline and in its practice. Revivals of normative theory include Rawls' (1971/1999) work on justice as the constitutive base of liberal democracy and, more recently, there has been an abundance of works in International Relations on the norms of humanitarian intervention, such as Wheeler's (2000) *Saving Strangers* thesis.

Researchers' normative 'leanings' influence their choice of theoretical approach even if they do not explicitly note this. This is inevitable, given that all political research is underpinned by normative considerations (Reus-Smit and Snidal, 2008: 7):

> We cannot answer the question of how we should act without some appreciation of the world in which we seek to act (the empirical) and some sense of what the goals are that we seek to achieve (the normative).

When using the research of others, then, we need to reflect on the implicit assumptions that underpin the work.

Theories can be placed within **paradigms** based on their specific onto-logical and epistemological assumptions. These paradigms tend to be competitive, advancing their own particular interpretations of data in accordance with their specific 'answers' to the 'Why?', 'How?' and 'What if?' questions that characterize political research. In International Relations, we can trace the evolution of the discipline via the theoretical debates between the main camps of scholars, **realism** versus liberalism, realism versus **behaviouralism**, realism versus pluralism versus radical-ism, **positivism** versus **post-positivism** and so on.

Debates occur not only between paradigms but also within them. Such debates are the engine of development within political research – we move from the thesis, to the antithesis, then the synthesis when the trajectory starts all over again. That said, some scholars refute the sug-gestion that any good can come from synthesizing theoretical approaches, especially if they believe that one of the approaches wants to absorb the other rather than unite in a mutually respectful union. This is especially the case for researchers whose theoretical stances have attained the status of orthodoxy within the discipline. In such cases, we can see that the 'desire to win, to stand one's ground perhaps not surprisingly, is most of the time stronger than the genuine search for an acceptable solution to the problem' (Kratochwil, 2003: 125).

Regardless of whether we welcome or reject the synthesis of theories, there will always be a diversity of theories within political research. This

theory

variety reflects the different ontological and epistemological positions of researchers, who perceive the political world and their role in it in different ways. Traditionally, International Relations is taught via the identification of comparisons between the competing paradigms of liberalism, realism and radicalism, respectively. This pedagogic practice allows students to better appreciate the contending ontologies of the different approaches and so aids the development of their own analysis. Theory is not simply something 'out there', however, something exogenous from our own internal thinking. It is not an 'optional extra' that we need to remember to bolt on to our research. Rather, it is a 'doing' exercise that allows us to engage reflectively and reflexively with our own research projects and the world in which we live. Learning 'how to think theoretically' is essential to meaningful scholarship as it denotes that we have (Rosenau and Durfee, 1995: 178):

> not a set of skills but rather a set of predispositions, a cluster of habits, a way of thinking, a mental lifestyle – or whatever may be the appropriate label of intellectual existence that governs the use of skills and the application of values.

FURTHER READING

Cox, R.W. (1981) 'Social forces, states and world orders', *Millennium – Journal of International Studies*, 10 (1): 126–55.

Kratochwil, F. (2003) 'The monologue of "science"', in G. Hellman (ed.), 'The forum: Are dialogue and synthesis possible in international relations', *International Studies Review*, 5: 124–8.

Rengger, N. and Thirkell-White, B. (2007) 'Still critical after all these years?: The past, present and future of critical theory in international relations', *Review of International Studies*, 33 (S1): 3–24.

Reus-Smit, C. and Snidal, D. (eds) (2008) 'Between Utopia and reality: The practical discourses of international relations', in C. Reus-Smit and D. Snidal (eds), *The Oxford Handbook of International Relations*. Oxford: Oxford University Press. pp. 3–58.

Rosenau, J. and Durfee, M. (1995) *Thinking Theory Thoroughly: Coherent approaches to an incoherent world*. Boulder, CO: Westview.

Savigny, H. and Marsden, L. (2011) *Doing Political Science and International Relations: Theories in action*. Houndmills, Basingstoke: Palgrave Macmillan.

Stoker, G. (1995) 'Introduction', in D. Marsh and G. Stoker, G. (eds), *Theory and Methods in Political Science*. Houndmills, Basingstoke: Palgrave Macmillan.

EXAMPLES

Fierke, K.M. and Jørgensen, K.E. (eds) (2001) *Constructing International Relations: The next generation*. Armonk, NY: M.E. Sharpe.

Keohane, R.O. (1989) *International Institutions and State Power: Essays in international relations theory*. Boulder, CO: Westview.

Rawls, J. (1971/1999) *A Theory of Justice*. Cambridge, MA: Harvard University Press.

Waltz, K. (1990) 'Realist thought and neorealist theory', *Journal of International Affairs*, 44 (1): 21–37.

Wheeler, N. (2000) *Saving Strangers: Humanitarian intervention in international society*. Oxford: Oxford University Press.

Williams, M. (2005) *The Realist Tradition and the Limits of International Relations*. Cambridge: Cambridge University Press.

Zacher, M.W. and Matthew, R.A (1995) 'Liberal international theory: Common threads, divergent strands', in C.W. Kegley (ed.), *Controversies in International Relations: Realism and the neoliberal challenge*. New York: St Martin's Press.

Triangulation

In reality, high-quality research is a constant battle and, empirically, we often face a gap between what we want to achieve ideally and what is actually attainable practically. Each method has strengths but also limitations, just as different types of data (quantitative and qualitative) capture different types of information. As such, high-quality research often equates to 'the best that is available', which is determined by two factors:

- the appropriateness of the research design
- the skills of the researcher – 'slavish adherence to particular methods carries few rewards' (Read and Marsh, 2002: 231).

In order to overcome the limitations of data type and method, researchers frequently employ a method of triangulation in order to increase confidence in their findings.

triangulation

Read and Marsh identify two key reasons for utilizing triangulation:

- one method alone may not allow us to address all aspects of the research question
- it increases the validity of the findings, by checking out the consistency of findings generated by different **methods** – 'all available techniques should be used to add power and sensitivity to individual judgement in understanding the environment being studied: "why throw away anything helpful?"' (Read and Marsh, 2002: 236).

One way in which we may 'mix' methodological approaches is to use different ones in different stages of research design – for example, large-scale surveys (which usually collect quantitative data) are often based on the findings of pilot studies (this may be a small number of interviews or **focus groups** in order to discover what the important **variables** might be or test whether or not participants understand what is being asked of them).

Denzin (1978) points to a difference between triangulation *within* methods – in which we use different tools to measure the same variable – and triangulation *between* methods – which is the combination of different methods, such as **surveys, interviewing, observation** and **documentary analysis**. The former is exemplified by survey research in which several questions are used to tap into complex variables (for example, British Election Studies surveys have used multiple questions to measure attitudes towards unemployment and jobs), though this type of triangulation is subject to the frailties of adopting a single methodological approach.

We do not have to search far to find examples of political research employing triangulated approaches – here are just a few. Vickers' (1995) research on the impact of the Cold War on the international trade union movement relied heavily on access to archival materials. The research combined evidence from historical documents with semistructured interviews conducted with academics and trade unionists, although this latter group proved to be most problematic because they were difficult to track down or were no longer alive (Vickers, 1995: 168). Ward and Gibson (1998) have taken a triangulated approach to understanding how political parties utilize the Internet in election campaigning (by also conducting qualitative interviews with the parties' Internet officials). Davies' (2001) research into security and intelligence services (a sensitive area), has found a barrier to data access in the form of the Official Secrets Act. According to Davies, official documentary archives (such as the Public Records Office) provide only 'sanitized' information (creating the problem of a top-down approach, plus incomplete documentation can provide a misleading picture). It proved necessary, therefore, to supplement the documentary research with interviews to 'enrich and interpret the arcane and often vaguely worded intelligence reviews, inquiries and legislation' (Davies, 2001: 74).

Read and Marsh (2002), however, identify potential problems with triangulation:

- using different approaches does not overcome the problem that researchers are likely to interpret data in different ways depending on their epistemological approach
- different approaches may produce different results.

In addition, Davies (2001) identifies the need to trade off sources in relation to the extent to which they can be trusted to be reliable – how do we weigh the importance of different sources of information? In Davies' case, he tends to prioritize written records over interviews and memoirs.

FURTHER READING

Denzin, N.K. (1978) *The Research Act: An introduction to sociological methods*. New York: McGraw-Hill.
Read, M. and Marsh, D. (2002) 'Combining qualitative and quantitative methods', in D. Marsh and G. Stoker (eds), *Theory and Methods in Political Science* (2nd edn). Houndmills, Basingstoke: Palgrave Macmillan.

EXAMPLES

Davies, P.H.J. (2001) 'Spies as informants: Triangulation and the interpretation of elite interview data in the study of the intelligence and security services', *Politics*, 21 (1): 73–80.
Vickers, R. (1995) 'Using archives in politics research', in P. Burnham (ed.), *Surviving the Research Process in Politics*. London: Pinter.
Ward, S. and Gibson, R. (1998) 'The first internet election?: UK political parties and campaigning in cyberspace', in I. Crewe, B. Gosschalk and J. Bartle (eds), *Political Communications: The general election campaign of 1997*. London: Frank Cass.

triangulation

To claim that our research is valid means that we have analysed what we claim to have analysed. This may seem a rather commonsense statement, but Politics and International Relations are based on some very broad, and often contested, terms, the nature of which are often subject to disagreements. As King et al. (2004: 191) note, political researchers tend to define and measure **concepts** with reference to examples:

> The advice methodologists usually give when hearing 'you know it when you see it' is to find a better, more precise theory and then measurement will be straightforward. This is the right advice, but it leads to a well-known problem in that highly concrete questions about big concepts … often produce more reliable measurements but not more valid ones.

As often abstract concepts are explained in political analysis, it is necessary to be absolutely clear about what is being analysed. This can be challenged in several ways.

First, when dealing with secondary data, it may be the case that a universal measure is not always used by each data-collection body. It is well-documented, for example, that official statistics are influenced by changing definitions and this poses challenges for comparisons made both across institutions and within the same organization over time. Take, for example, the concept of 'democratic'. As researchers, we all have ideas about what a democratic state might include, in terms of institutions, rules and practices, but where do we draw the fine line between democratic and undemocratic? Bowman et al. (2005: 940) focus on the use of long-term cross-national scales to compare the measurement of 'political democracy' in five Central American countries and the extent to which validity may be compromised by data-induced measurement error:

> This kind of error occurs when analysts incorrectly code cases because of limitations in the underlying data on which they rely as descriptions of empirical reality. Typically, data-induced measurement error grows out of the use of inaccurate, partial, or misleading secondary sources.

key research concepts in politics & international relations

The practical solution to this, they argue, is to use area experts in coding cases.

Second, often proxy, **variables** are used as indicators. When considering the human rights record of a country, there is not actually a physical presence called 'human rights'. Rather, we look to indicators that we think contribute to human rights, such as freedom of speech, the right to a fair trial, freedom from slavery. Focusing on only certain proxy measures might produce very different research outcomes. As Hopkin (2002: 259) states, 'conceptual vagueness and inconsistency pose a serious threat to the validity of empirical generalisations about the relationship between … variables.'

In order to ensure validity, there are numerous steps we can take (Seale and Filmer, 1998: 134):

> The first and most common method is known as face validity, whereby the researcher thinks hard about whether the questions indicate the intended concept. The assessment of face validity may be helped by asking people with practical or professional knowledge of the area to assess how well questions indicate the concept … Criterion validity involves comparing the results of questions with established indicators of the same concept … Construct validity evaluates a measure according to how well it conforms to expectations derived from theory.

In exploring the issue of **ethics** in leadership, Morrell and Hartley (2006) address the issue of measuring the skills of local political leaders. In order to develop the Warwick Political Leadership Questionnaire so that it could offer **reliability** and validity, the research team used a four-stage development process. Face validity was addressed at the second stage via **focus groups** and workshops with 'elected members, informed commentators (e.g. senior council officers, senior police officers, chairs of housing associations, senior health service managers) and other parties (e.g. academic colleagues) to explore the notion of effective political leadership, and to generate a list of core capabilities, contextual factors, and key challenges faced by leaders, as well as to develop and test in an iterative fashion items designed to tap these dimensions' (Morrell and Hartley, 2006: 61). The centrality of the target population and related experts is evidenced. Construct validity was addressed in the third stage, in which a pilot of the questionnaire was tested out on a small but reasonably diverse group of councillors, enabling the removal of weak items.

validity

Researchers tend to focus on two further aspects of validity. If a study holds internal validity, we have confidence that the objectives are achieved. If, for example, we wished to map trends in political participation, we need to ensure that we have developed an appropriate conceptual framework as to what political participation means. External validity reflects our ability to generalize. Claims that are valid in relation to a particular age group, country or social class may not be applicable to all. In their review of studies using process analysis and process evaluation (with specific reference to healthcare), Calnan and Ferlie (2003: 191) assert that:

> A common objection to process analysis (along with other forms of qualitative research) is that although it may be interesting or 'truthful' (that is, possess high internal validity), it is based on small numbers of interviews, or a restricted number of sites, or that it derives only local lessons. These concerns about the low level of external validity associated with process research may also make it less credible in the policy arena where a broad empirical basis may be more persuasive.

In order for research outcomes to be valid, it must also be established that they are **reliable**.

FURTHER READING

Hopkin, J. (2002) 'Comparative methods', in D. Marsh and G. Stoker (eds), *Theory and Methods in Political Science* (2nd edn). Houndmills, Basingstoke: Palgrave Macmillan.

Seale, C.F. and Filmer, P. (1998) 'Doing social surveys', in C.F. Seale (ed.), *Researching Society and Culture*. London: Sage.

EXAMPLES

Bowman, K., Lehoucq, F. and Mahoney, J. (2005) 'Measuring political democracy: Case expertise, data adequacy, and Central America', *Comparative Political Studies*, 38 (8): 939–70.

Calnan, M. and Ferlie, E. (2003) 'Analysing process in healthcare: The methodological and theoretical challenges', *Policy & Politics*, 31 (2): 185–93.

King, G., Murray, C.J.L., Salomon, J.A. and Tandon, A. (2004) 'Enhancing the validity and cross-cultural comparability of measurement in survey research', *American Political Science Review*, 98 (1): 191–207.

Morrell, K. and Hartley, J. (2006) 'Ethics in leadership: The case of local politicians', *Local Government Studies*, 32 (1): 55–70.

Variables

> A variable is something that varies: it is a phenomenon that assumes different (varying) values according to different cases ... In the experimental methods we can make values vary by manipulating reality. In the social sciences, this is often not possible: we cannot artificially change the sex of a person, increase his age, and so on. We therefore need to create variation by taking many different cases with different values, according to a number of properties (variables). (Moses and Knutsen, 2007: 76)

The term 'variable' is a classic example of a technical term we use as researchers that is not in everyday usage. Rather than use vague language, such as 'things', 'influences', 'changes' or 'factors', we refer to research variables. For example, political participation may be referred to as a variable as it it can be defined in a way that makes it clear to others what we mean by the term which is classified by boundaries – that is, it should be clear whether an observable phenomenon is defined as political participation or not (though the boundaries themselves may be subject to different definitions). Variables are an important aspect of conducting clear research as they allow us to isolate component parts of much broader phenomena.

We can understand the relationship between variables by considering the concepts of 'civil society' and 'democratization'. 'Civil society' has become a much-used phrase in political and international relations research in the latter part of the twentieth century. As Sardamov (2005: 380) states:

> Much of the scholarly literature, as well as policy papers and grant proposals, posit a strong correlation between the strength of civil society and democratization. Such findings are assumed to imply a causal relationship between civil society and democracy. Building a robust civil society is therefore postulated as a precondition for democratization and democratic consolidation. In fact, the correlation between 'civil society' and democracy may be spurious, both phenomena being shaped by deeper social processes related to modernization and individualization.

We can see from Sardamov's argument that there are two concerns regarding the attempt to link the variables of civil society with democracy and democratization. First, it may enable those with power to establish clear boundaries as to what is and what is not acceptable in 'civil society', in the sense that there are established 'right' and 'wrong' means by which democracy can be achieved. Second, and we will come to this shortly, it could in fact be the case that democracy is enhanced by social processes other than civil society, but, as the two appear to occur together in observable cases, we make a spurious **observation**. This could also be related to non-political examples of ritualistic behaviour. For example, in some Westernized societies, the superstition of saluting a single magpie is widespread, in the belief that sighting a single magpie is bad luck. It would be difficult to evidence that the absence of bad luck is down to someone's superstitious behaviour.

Two basic types of variables can be identified – the *independent* variable and the *dependent* variable. An independent variable is an explanatory variable (say, for example, someone's age, sex, level of education, occupation), while the dependent variable is what we are trying to explain (in our case, political participation). If each of our independent variables were, in fact, relevant, then a change in their character would lead to a change in the dependent variable. For example, we might find that those who participate in politics the most are older, well-educated and in full-time employment, while those who are least likely to participate politically are young, lack qualifications and are unemployed.

Rarely in political research is a phenomenon simply explained by a simple independent and dependent variable. We may indeed find that those over the age of 65 participate in politics more frequently than those who are 18, but does this mean there is some 'participation hormone' which only takes effect as we age? Probably not. It may be that those over 65 participate more because they are retired and have more spare time than the young or they have had more opportunities over time to join organizations and bond with like-minded others. 'Free time' could, in this case, be an *intervening* variable – that is, it has an effect on the relationship between the independent and dependent variables. If the relationship between age and political participation was nothing more than a coincidence with no real explanatory value, then we would refer to age as a *spurious* variable – hence Sardamov's suggestion that civil society is a spurious indicator of democracy.

In their study of Internet polling in the 2001 British Election Study, Sanders et al. (2004) discovered that varying **sampling** approaches (notably probability and net sampling) led to differing profiles – namely, they differed in terms of their projected vote shares, demographics and partisan orientations. By testing a simple model (Labour voting), they were able to show that, despite the substantively different demographic and attitudinal profiles, the extent to which erroneous **inferences** might be drawn was limited. Although a zero erroneous effect would be the most desirable outcome, they deemed this a satisfactory level of performance – and that there was methodological justification for utilizing net polling in public opinion research.

FURTHER READING

Moses, J.W. and Knutsen, T.L. (2007) *Ways of Knowing: Competing methodologies in social and political research*. Houndmills, Basingstoke: Palgrave Macmillan.

EXAMPLES

Sanders, D., Clarke, H., Stewart, M. and Whiteley, P. (2004) 'The 2001 British election study internet poll', *Journal of Political Marketing*, 3 (4): 29–55.
Sardamov, I. (2005) '"Civil society" and the limits of democratic assistance', *Government and Opposition*, 40 (3): 379–402.

variables

index

key research concepts in
politics & international relations

index

index